D1284250

A Practical Guide to
Staff
Development

Evidence-Based Tools and Techniques
for Effective Education

Adrianne E. Avillion, DEd, RN

HCPro

Adrianne E. Avillion, DEd, RN, Author
Emily Sheahan, Group Publisher
Rebecca Hendren, Senior Managing Editor
Lindsey Cardarelli, Associate Editor
Janell Lukac, Layout Artist
Crystal Beland, Layout Artist

Leah Tracosas, Copyeditor
Patrick Campagnone, Cover Designer
Liza Banks, Proofreader
Darren Kelly, Books Production Supervisor
Susan Darbyshire, Art Director
Jean St. Pierre, Director of Operations

Advice given is general. Readers should consult professional counsel for specific legal, ethical, or clinical questions. Arrangements can be made for quantity discounts. For more information, contact:

HCPro, Inc.
75 Sylvan Street, Suite A-101
Danvers, MA 01923
Telephone: 800/650-6787 or 781/639-1872
Fax: 781/639-2982
E-mail: *customerservice@hcpro.com*

Visit HCPro at: *www.hcpro.com* and *www.hcmarketplace.com*

Table of contents

List of figures

About the author

Adrianne E. Avillion, DEd, RN

Adrianne E. Avillion, DEd, RN, is the owner of Avillion's Curriculum Design in York, PA. She specializes in designing continuing education programs for healthcare professionals and freelance medical writing. She also offers consulting services in work redesign, quality improvement, and staff development.

Avillion has published extensively. She is the author of the first edition of *A Practical Guide to Staff Development: Tools and Techniques for Effective Education* and served as the editor of the first and second editions of *The Core Curriculum for Staff Development*. Her most recent publications include *Evidence-Based Staff Development: Strategies to Create, Measure, and Refine Your Program* and *Designing Nursing Orientation: Evidence-Based Strategies for Effective Programs*, both published by HCPro, Inc. in Marblehead, MA, and *Nurse Entrepreneurship: The Art of Running Your Own Business*, published by Creative Health Care Management in Minneapolis, MN. She is also a frequent presenter at conferences and conventions devoted to the specialty of continuing education and staff development.

Introduction

Just a few short years ago I asked myself, "Why doesn't someone write a really practical book about staff development?" I wanted a resource that was easy to read and filled with practical tips and suggestions. I asked the healthcare editors at HCPro if they were interested in just such a project. Their response was, "Yes! Go ahead and write it!" I was thrilled to have the chance to do so, and thus the first edition of *A Practical Guide to Staff Development* became a reality.

Since the publication of the first edition, the practice of staff development has grown in stature and importance. Staff development specialists continue to function as leaders and innovators and are an indispensable resource to their organizations.

This second edition identifies evidence-based staff development practice as the foundation for the delivery of staff development products and services. Strategies from needs assessment and program planning to implementation and evaluation focus on the need to produce evidence that links education to organizational effectiveness.

This book is jam-packed with practical information, tools, and templates designed to make your life as a staff development specialist easier. It also includes a CD-ROM from which you can download various charts and tools and personalize them as your own.

It is my hope that this book will serve as a truly useful resource and facilitate your ability to add to the body of knowledge of staff development practice.

—*Adrianne E. Avillion, DEd, RN*

How to use the files on your CD-ROM

The following file names correspond with figures listed in the book *A Practical Guide to Staff Development: Evidence-Based Tools and Techniques for Effective Education, Second Edition.*

Fig2-1.doc   Figure 2.1: Sample values statement

Fig2-2.doc   Figure 2.2: Sample vision statement #1

Fig2-3.doc   Figure 2.3: Sample vision statement #2

Fig2-4.doc   Figure 2.4: Recommendations for crafting a vision

Fig2-5.doc   Figure 2.5: Sample mission statement

Fig2-6.doc   Figure 2.6: Characteristics of a mission statement

Fig2-7.doc   Figure 2.7: Sample goal and corresponding objectives

Fig4-1.doc   Figure 4.1: Sample competencies

Fig6-1.doc   Figure 6.1: Implementing adult learning principles

Fig7-1.doc   Figure 7.1: Learning styles cheat sheet

Fig7-2.doc   Figure 7.2: Left-brain learners vs. right-brain learners

Fig8-1.doc   Figure 8.1: Multigeneration teaching

Fig9-1.doc   Figure 9.1: Diversity education planner

Fig11-1.doc   Figure 11.1: EBP analysis template

Fig11-2.doc   Figure 11.2: Strategies for audiovisuals

Fig12-1.doc   Figure 12.1: Sample template for evaluating distance learning

Fig13-1.doc   Figure 13.1: Levels of expertise for the staff development specialist

Fig14-1.doc   Figure 14.1: Sample needs-assessment form

Fig14-2.doc   Figure 14.2: Organization of needs-assessment data

Fig15-1.doc   Figure 15.1: Template for orientation analysis

Fig15-2.doc   Figure 15.2: Orientation data collection

Fig17-1.doc   Figure 17.1: Template for policy/regulation inservice documentation

Fig17-2.doc   Figure 17.2: Inservice documentation form for new equipment

Fig19-1.doc   Figure 19.1: Program analysis template

Fig20-1.doc   Figure 20.1: Classroom evaluation form

Fig20-2.doc   Figure 20.2: Distance learning evaluation form

Fig21-1.doc   Figure 21.1: Demonstration of competency achievement form

Fig22-1.doc   Figure 22.1: Evaluation of behavior (applied knowledge)

Fig23-1.doc   Figure 23.1: Administrative report on staff development EBP

To adapt any of the files to your own facility, simply follow the instructions below to open the CD.

If you have trouble reading the forms, click on "View," and then "Normal." To adapt the forms, save them first to your own hard drive or disk (by clicking "File," then "Save as," and changing the system to your own). Then change the information to fit your facility, and add or delete any items that you wish to change.

Installation instructions

This product was designed for the Windows operating system and includes Word files that will run under Windows 95/98 or greater. The CD will work on all PCs and most Macintosh systems. To run the files on the CD/ROM, take the following steps:

1. Insert the CD into your CD/ROM drive.

2. Double-click on the "My Computer" icon, next double-click on the CD drive icon.

3. Double-click on the files you wish to open.

4. Adapt the files by moving the cursor over the areas you wish to change, highlighting them, and typing in the new information using Microsoft Word.

5. To save a file to your facility's system, click on "File" and then click on "Save As." Select the location where you wish to save the file and then click on "Save."

6. To print a document, click on "File" and then click on "Print."

Unit 1

Foundations of
Staff Development

Chapter 1

Evolution of staff development

Learning Objectives

After reading this chapter, the participant will be able to:

- Describe the historical evolution of staff development

- Differentiate between traditional and contemporary staff development practice

Staff development is the process of providing continuing education and training for people who work in organizations that specialize in the delivery of healthcare products and services. Historically, staff development departments were staffed by nurses for the purpose of conducting orientation and on-the-job training for members of the nursing department. Today, however, staff development departments are staffed by a variety of disciplines and are often responsible for the delivery of educational products and services to entire hospitals and healthcare systems. Staff development specialists are also responsible for evaluating not only the effectiveness of their services, but the effect such services have on organizational success. To accomplish this, evidence-based practice must guide the delivery of staff development practice.

Its Origin

Nursing staff development began with Florence Nightingale's efforts to establish training schools for nurses and to improve the efficiency of care delivery in hospitals. Nightingale encouraged nurses to embark on a journey of lifelong learning and use their knowledge to improve patient care. However, there were few formal

staff development programs for nurses in the late 1800s and early 1900s (Avillion 1998, Nightingale 1859, Tobin et al 1974).

In the 1920s and 30s, the Great Depression forced many nurses into the hospital setting for the first
time since their initial training. Prior to the Depression, most nurses earned their living as private-
duty nurses in private practice, and nursing students provided the majority of care to hospitalized
patients. However, the Depression drastically decreased the number of people who could afford
private care. Hospital administrators found themselves hiring graduate nurses to work in the
hospital setting (Avillion 1998, DeSilets et al 2004, Tobin et al 1974).

This shift in practice triggered the need for various staff development services. Newly hired nurses
required orientation to hospital routines, procedures, policies, equipment, and regulations. These
nurses had to learn to function as members of a team who care for large numbers of patients rather
than as individual practitioners who care for only one patient at a time. Educational emphasis was
on orientation to the hospital setting and inservice training for on-the-job skills (Avillion 1998,
DeSilets at al 2004, Tobin et al 1974).

The advent of World War II brought more changes to the profession. Nurses left hospitals in large
numbers to join the armed forces, causing a shortage of active nurses at home. As a result, the
number of nonprofessional staff increased in an effort to compensate for the lack of registered
nurses. In many cases, inactive nurses returned to hospitals to help deal with the shortage. Thus
refresher courses became part of staff development responsibilities. Training, inservice, and continuing education for nonprofessional staff added to the services provided by staff development specialists (Avillion 1998, Brunt et al 2001, DeSilets at al 2004, Tobin et al 1974).

In the 1940s and 50s, nurses and other healthcare personnel began to evaluate their responsibilities
and necessary qualifications using the standards being set by various professional organizations. In
1953, the Joint Commission for the Improvement of Care of the Patient proposed that a distinct
department devoted to the training and continuing education of the nursing department be established. Leadership and management training became part of the staff development role in the 1960s
as the need for administrative skills became more apparent. Objective, scientific evaluation of
nursing care delivery using documented standards of quality became important not only for patients' well-being, but also to establish how and why nursing is practiced. In 1969, the Medical
College of Virginia's Health Sciences Division of Virginia Commonwealth University sponsored the

first national conference on continuing education for nurses (Avillion 1998, Brunt et al 2001, DeSilets at al 2004, Tobin et al 1974).

Specialty Status

Several critical events pertaining to the establishment of staff development as a distinct healthcare specialty occurred in the 1970s:

- **1970:** The *Journal of Continuing Education in Nursing* was published.

- **1973:** The American Nurses Association (ANA) established the Council on Continuing Education.

- **1974:** The *Process of Staff Development: Components for Change* was published, which defined the practice of staff development until the 1980s.

- **1978:** The ANA published *Guidelines for Staff Development.*

- **1978:** The Joint Commission on Accreditation of Hospitals mandated that a position to oversee and coordinate staff development activities be established in its affiliated hospitals.

Part of the Business Plan

The viewpoint that healthcare is truly a business was acknowledged by both healthcare personnel and consumers during the 1980s. The need for education pertaining to financial management and the business aspects of healthcare became essential as the industry moved toward the for-profit sector. The following 1980s events show that staff development was increasingly being viewed as both a necessity and a specialty within the healthcare arena:

- **1985:** The *Journal of Nursing Staff Development* (now known as the *Journal for Nurses in Staff Development*) was published.

- **1989:** The National Nursing Staff Development Organization (NNSDO) was established.

- Over the decade, several books devoted to the practice of nursing staff development were published.

Credentialing

During the 1990s, rapid advances in technology and the prevention and treatment of disease triggered the need for lifelong learning among all who work in the healthcare field. These advances also clarified the need for properly credentialed, experienced staff development specialists. Highlights of the 1990s include the following:

- **1992:** The ANA published *Roles and Responsibilities for Nursing Continuing Education and Staff Development Across All Settings.*

- **1992:** The American Nurses Credentialing Center offered the first certification examination for nursing continuing education and staff development.

- **1995:** The first *Core Curriculum for Nursing Staff Development* was published.

- Throughout the decade, many staff development departments' responsibilities expanded to include the provision of education for entire hospitals and health systems, including multisite organizations.

- Emphasis shifted from provision of services to evaluating how education affects organizational effectiveness.

- The term *staff development* was replaced in some organizations with other terms such as *organizational development, corporate university, education department, and professional development department.*

- Qualifications for leadership in staff development focused on educational and managerial expertise rather than clinical expertise.

Today and Beyond

The 21st century brings a new era of challenges and excitement for staff development specialists. Nursing shortages occur with frightening regularity. But despite such shortages, healthcare professionals are expected to provide safe and appropriate care. Let's look at some of the most obvious changes by comparing traditional staff development services to those of the 21st century:

Then: In the late 1970s, physical assessment skills (e.g., heart and lung auscultation) were new, trendy topics. Continuing education classes focused on acquiring and developing these skills.

Now: These skills are the norm, not the exception.

Then: Clinical expertise was the primary criterion to leadership promotion.

Now: The focus on clinical expertise has been replaced by a focus on the need for strong administrative, financial, and leadership skills.

Then: Twenty years ago, most inservice and continuing education offerings were held during the day in formal classroom settings.

Now: Education is offered around the clock, often via distance-learning techniques such as computer-based learning (CBL) and self-learning activities.

Then: The burden of responsibility for learning was placed on staff development specialists. They were accountable for the willingness (or lack thereof) of the learners to learn.

Now: The learner is responsible for his or her own knowledge acquisition. An emphasis is put on lifelong learning.

Then: As recently as the 1980s, education evaluation focused on the number of participants who attended a program, learner satisfaction, and the number of programs offered monthly.

Now: Educators look at the "big picture." In other words, how does the provision of education affect organizational performance?

Then: The staff development specialist's role was solely that of educator.

Now: The staff development specialist assumes multiple roles in addition to that of educator, including researcher, consultant, change agent, manager, and performance coach.

Then: Traditionally, staff development specialists focused teaching skills on classroom learning.

Now: They are expected to be experts in a variety of teaching methods, particularly distance learning and CBL.

Then: Accreditation concerns emphasized JCAHO (now known as The Joint Commission) standards and perhaps a specialty accreditation (e.g., CARF-Commission on Accreditation of Rehabilitation Facilities).

Now: Accreditation concerns cover a broad area in addition to The Joint Commission standards, including specialty accreditations such as rehabilitation and trauma. Staff development specialists are generally responsible for assisting with self-survey processes and offering education pertaining to successful accreditation achievement.

Two concepts deserve special attention: how nursing shortages impact the practice of staff development and how staff development specialists measure the impact of their products and services.

Nursing Shortages

Staffing problems have always been (and will always be) a concern in healthcare organizations. However, the reasons for these problems vary according to supply and demand and fluctuating work environments.

Even during times when an adequate number of nurses seek employment, staffing problems exist. During such times, some healthcare organizations keep staffing to a minimum in a misguided attempt to save money, thus creating unsatisfactory and even dangerous working conditions. In the past, as career opportunities for women grew, the number of people entering the nursing profession decreased. Healthcare organizations responded (and continue to respond in some cases) with frantic quick-fix solutions, such as sign-on bonuses and the offer of 12-hour workdays in exchange for shorter work weeks. However, these attempts failed. Nurses began to job hop in the pursuit of sign-on bonuses and other perks, thus costing organizations increasing amounts of money, not only in the form of bonuses, but also in the form of orientations for nurses who stay with an organization just long enough to collect hiring perks.

The practice of 12-hour workdays is beginning to draw fire from researchers. The fatigue that occurs when working long hours is associated with an increase in the number of adverse occurrences. Also, as the nursing population ages, extended work hours become problematic. The average age of RNs in the United States is 46.8 years, with just more than 41% over 50 years of age and only 8% under the age of 30 (U.S. Department of Health and Human Services 2004).

How do these statistics affect staff development? Staffing shortages in nursing and other healthcare specialties trigger a number of educational needs. However, these needs should not be implemented in a knee-jerk manner. For example, shortages often spark an outcry for frequent rapid orientation sessions that send inadequately prepared new employees into the work setting, leading to resentment and confusion for both the new employees and more tenured staff, and increasing the possibility of medical errors. Think about meeting these needs in a way based on best practices that enhances educational outcomes not only during staffing shortages, but also on a long-term basis. Here are some needs that will persist for years to come:

- Delivery of flexible, fast, and efficient education services based on evidence that helps to identify best practices in staff development

- Implementation of blended learning formats to meet educational needs in efficient and cost-effective manners

- Development of a flexible orientation program that takes into account the background and experience of employees

Impact of Staff Development Practice

Staff development practice has come a long way from the days when success was measured by how many persons attended a given education program or how many programs were offered within a specific time frame. Today, it is imperative that staff development specialists be able to provide evidence that their offerings positively impact organizational effectiveness. To do this, evidence must be gathered showing an association between education and outcomes pertaining to entities such as accreditation status, job performance, and patient outcomes.

Benchmarks and best practices in staff development must be used as guides when developing and implementing products and services. This mandates that evidence-based practice, a given in clinical services, become part of staff development practice as well. Evidence-based practice in staff development should include:

- Evaluation of current products and services for their effectiveness

- Identification of best practices in staff development based on evidence

- Evaluation of how staff development products and services are being delivered in light of best practices

- Establishment of a mechanism for incorporating research into staff development practice

As healthcare evolves, so do the roles and responsibilities of staff development specialists. The only certainty in healthcare is that change is, and will continue to be, constant. Staff development specialists must be experts in adaptation to provide educational resources that help ensure that the quality of patient care remains safe, appropriate, and of high quality. To meet this challenge, staff development departments must establish sound operational foundations based on evidence of best practices and benchmarks.

References

1. Avillion, A. 1998. The *Redesign of Nursing Staff Development*. Pensacola, FL: The National Nursing Staff Development Organization (NNSDO).

2. Brunt, B., Pack, J., and Parr, P. 2001. "The history of staff development." In A. Avillion (Ed.), *Core Curriculum for Staff Development*. 2nd ed. Pensacola, FL: NNSDO. 3–17.

3. DeSilets, L., and Pinkerton, S., 2004. Looking back on 25 years of continuing education. *The Journal of Continuing Education in Nursing* 35(1): 12–13.

4. Nightingale, F. 1859. *Notes on Nursing*. London: Harrison and Sons.

5. Tobin, H., Yoder, P., Hull, P., and Scott, B. 1974. *The Process of Staff Development: Components for Change*. St. Louis: Mosby.

6. U.S. Department of Health and Human Services. 2004. *The registered nurse population: Findings from the 2004 national sample survey of registered nurses*. Retrieved February 17, 2008 from *http://bhpr.hrsa.gov/healthworkforce/msurvey04*.

Chapter 2

Mission, vision, and values: Relying on EBP

Learning Objectives

After reading this chapter, the participant will be able to:

- Implement strategic planning using mission, vision, and values statements
- Determine realistic departmental goals
- Determine realistic objectives that correlate with departmental goals

Strategic Planning

Do you believe that strategic planning depends on well-crafted and implemented mission, vision, and values? Do you think mission, vision, and values statements are important? Do they guide your staff development practice? Or do you consider them just a "paper exercise"? If you answered "yes" to the last question, then the information in this section is especially important for you to understand.

Strategic planning is the process of determining an organization's (or department's) direction. It guides the way products and services are developed and delivered and how resources (including employees and capital) are allocated and utilized. In healthcare organizations, products and services revolve around patient care needs. Strategic planning focuses on facilitating the best possible patient outcomes in an efficent, cost-effective manner (Avillion 2003, Avillion 2007, Tiffany et al 1997).

Successful strategic planning depends on:

- Complete and active support from administration, management, and staff

- Effective, truthful communication

- Organizationwide acknowledgement of the need for strategic planning

Staff development products and services must be developed to enhance job performance and patient outcomes according to the mission, vision, and values of the organization within which they exist (Avillion 2003). The staff development mission, vision, and values statements establish a foundation for the delivery of education. You must write statements that appropriately guide how you deliver your department's products and services in accordance with the organization's statements. Successful departmental strategic planning depends on:

- Thorough and active support from the director of staff development

- Thorough and active support from the members of the staff development department

- Effective, truthful communication among members of the staff development department and between the staff development department and the rest of the organization

- Acknowledgement by all members of the staff development department of the need for strategic planning (About.com 2007 *How to implement strategic planning*)

When crafting your mission, vision, and values statements, consider how you will use evidence of staff development best practices to plan strategically. Evidence-based practice (EBP) is the process of making clinical decisions based on the most current and valid research. The goal of EBP is to improve patient outcomes.

In staff development, EBP is the process of using benchmarks and best practice evidence to close the gap between actual staff development practice and the identified best practices (Avillion 2007). EBP must be part of your strategic planning, and as such, its terminology must be reflected in your mission, vision, and values.

This section of the chapter defines the terms *values, vision,* and *mission.* Templates to help you write practical, usable statements are also provided, as well as recommendations to help you write corresponding goals. All are written from the perspective of EBP in staff development.

Values

A values statement (referred to as a *philosophy* by some organizations) is a set of beliefs and principles that guide your department's activities to achieve a specific purpose. These values must be stated clearly and succinctly and should guide your department's response when unexpected challenges arise (Avillion 2003, Brunt 2001, Tiffany et al 1997). All members of the staff development department must not only understand and agree with identified values, but also take an active part in crafting the values themselves.

Note that the values of all employees, combined with their experience, upbringing, culture, and moral beliefs, form the organizational and departmental culture. For an organization or department to live their values, the following must take place:

- All employees must model the identified values in how they perform their jobs, how they make decisions, and how they interact with each other and customers (e.g., patients, physicians, families, etc.).

- Values must be used to help establish work-related priorities.

- Values must guide the decision-making process.

- Recruitment and retention efforts should focus on hiring and promoting persons whose behaviors are congruent with established values (About.com 2007 *Build a strategic framework*).

A values statement like the one in Figure 2.1 (found on the CD-ROM included with this book) can be written only in conjunction with the organization's values statement. When writing your values statement, make sure you have a copy of your organization's values statement in front of you. If administration does not agree and overtly support staff development values, you will find it difficult, if not impossible, to achieve your goals and objectives.

In fact, two of the top reasons for education failures are due to administrative:

1. Lack of commitment to and involvement with the education process

2. Failure to hold participants accountable for their own learning (Phillips et al 2002)

Include language in your statement that addresses these issues; it is integral. Unfortunately, most staff development specialists experience both factors at some point during their careers. Therefore, work closely with administrators and managers when developing your values statement. If you absolutely cannot agree on values, consider finding employment at another organization—one whose values coincide with yours.

Pay attention to the commitment to EBP in staff development. Ensure that:

- The commitment is made by the staff development department, as well as by organizational leadership

- The importance of keeping abreast of current staff development research findings and conducting such research is clearly spelled out

- The values statement also acknowledges that the staff development specialists within this organization have an obligation to contribute to the body of knowledge that comprises staff development practice

Vision

Your vision is an image of what you want your department's future to be. It must be precise, easily understood, and well-written. Your vision must be clear not only to those within the staff development department, but to those who use your products and services. Your vision should pull the staff development department employees together as they strive to build a common identity and future (Brunt 2001, Tiffany et al 1997). A well-crafted vision statement is:

- Driven by your values

- Future oriented

- Realistic

- Inspiring

- Concise

Visions must be realistic. A vision that has national implications is probably not achievable if you work in a small community hospital. The vision should inspire staff to work to their maximum abilities, yet realize that it must also be attainable. An unrealistic vision will discourage more than it motivates. But a vision that is realistic, exciting, attainable, and demanding triggers feelings of pride and enthusiasm among employees (About.com 2007 *Build a strategic framework*).

Figures 2.2 and 2.3 are sample vision statements that include specific staff development EBP components. Figure 2.4 offers specific recommendations for writing a vision statement.

Figure 2.2

Sample vision statement #1

Children's City Hospital Staff Development Department

It is the vision of the staff development department to be a statewide leader in the provision of education programs that focus on excellence in pediatric healthcare services and to conduct staff development research for the purpose of identifying statewide best practices in continuing education in pediatrics.

Figure 2.3

Sample vision statement #2

American Rehabilitation System Education Department

It is the vision of the education department of the American Rehabilitation System to be a national leader of professional staff development and continuing education dedicated to excellence in physical medicine and rehabilitation products and services. Included in this vision is the identification of benchmarks that guide excellence in the provision of such products and services.

Figure 2.4

Recommendations for crafting a vision

1. Determine the department's strengths and weaknesses.
2. Determine what is inspirational and what is realistic.
3. When writing your vision, consider the following questions:
   - What does the organization expect education and training to accomplish?
   - What does the staff development department expect education and training to accomplish?
   - How does the staff development department contribute to the quality and appropriateness of patient care?
   - How does the staff development department support the organization's financial plan?
   - Does this vision complement the values of the staff development department and the organization?
   - Does this vision stem from your organizational vision?
   - What role does research play in departmental activities? How will staff development research data be used to improve staff development practice?
4. Incorporate your vision statement in all departmental activities, including but not limited to needs assessments, program planning and implementation, quality improvement activities, research endeavors, and performance evaluations.
5. Evaluate your vision statement regularly.

Mission

The mission must clearly communicate the purpose and direction of staff development activities to persons within and outside of the department. It describes essential functions as well as the overall reason for the department's existence.

It is important that your mission statement reflect the importance of and your commitment to EBP in staff development. References to EBP in your mission statement might include:

- The importance of gathering data from a variety of sources

- Data used as evidence to justify staff development activities

- Showing that the need for evidence supports the need for staff development research

Ultimately, anyone reading your mission statement should be able to recognize that your staff development practice is based on evidence.

The mission statement in Figure 2.5 clearly focuses on an area of great organizational importance: The organization is made up of five freestanding rehabilitation facilities. If something is important to your organization, it is important to you. Do not write a mission statement that conflicts with your organization's mission.

Figure 2.5

Sample mission statement

The staff development department of the Hazelwood Healthcare System upholds the mission, vision, and values of the organization by developing and offering educational products and services crafted to improve the quality and appropriateness of patient care.

Educational products and services enhance organizational effectiveness by providing programming designed to increase knowledge and skills of employees. The staff development department facilitates the maintenance of Commission on Accreditation of Rehabilitation Facilities (CARF) standards for the organization's five freestanding physical-medicine and rehabilitation hospitals by designing products and services specific to the needs of rehabilitation staff.

The staff development department is committed to analyzing research data to identify benchmarks and best practices in the staff development field. In addition to reviewing research conducted by persons external to Hazelwood Healthcare System, the staff development department is committed to initiating its own research endeavors and to sharing the results of these endeavors with the organization and with the community of staff development specialists on a national level.

Suppose your organization has recently purchased several long-term-care facilities. You are excited about the possibility of developing education for staff members who work with a geriatric population; however, your administration has decided to outsource educational activities for these new acquisitions and wants you to concentrate on facilitating trauma center accreditation at various sites within the system. In fact, your organization's vision is to become a national leader in trauma care. No matter how much you believe that long-term-care education should be a priority for your department, emphasizing it in your departmental mission or values is a mistake because it conflicts with organizational emphasis.

Use the characteristics of a mission statement detailed in Figure 2.6 when you write your mission statement. Note that the importance of research is mentioned in both the sample mission statement and the characteristics of a well-written mission statement.

Figure 2.6

Characteristics of a mission statement

The mission statement must:

- Reflect departmental and organizational values and vision
- Reflect—never contradict—the organization's mission
- Identify what the staff development department does for the organization
- Identify appropriate ways of incorporating EBP as the foundation for staff development
- Focus on both organizational and departmental priorities
- Serve as the foundation for departmental goals and objectives
- Be reviewed regularly and revised as organizational priorities evolve and change

Goals

Goals are broadly written statements that identify what a department should accomplish within a specified period of time. They interpret the mission statement into the intentions that direct the department's activities. Departmental goals must be based on relevant organizational goals, linking the provision of education to organizational business goals. The plan to achieve each goal consists of measurable, realistic objectives. Objectives must identify who is responsible for their achievement and within what time frame the objectives must be achieved. Objectives guide the delegation of work within the department (Avillion 2003, Brunt 2001, Tiffany et al 1997).

Let's return to the mission statement in Figure 2.5 from the fictitious Hazlewood Healthcare System and develop a goal and objectives based on this mission.

Notice that the goals in Figure 2.7 stem from both organizational priorities and the departmental mission statement. The objectives are measurable, identify person(s) responsible, and include a deadline for achievement.

Figure 2.7

Sample goal and corresponding objectives

Goal: Achieve CARF accreditation for freestanding physical rehabilitation facilities within Hazlewood Healthcare System.

Objective	Responsibility	Deadline
1. Review CARF standards pertaining to education and summarize them for staff-development department and the managers and staff of the rehabilitation facilities.	S. Sanders, RN, MEd P. Davis, PT, MEd	10/14/2008
2. Delegate responsibility for specific education activities at identified rehabilitation facilities.	A. Mendel, RN, DEd, Director, staff development	10/14/2008
3. Evaluate current adherence to CARF education standards and formulate action plan to improve/maintain adherence.	A. Mendel, RN, DEd, S. Sanders, RN, MEd P. Davis, PT, MEd	10/31/2008
4. Conduct a literature review for the purpose of identifying best practices in the delivery of continuing education pertaining to spinal cord injuries.	S. Sanders, RN, Med.	10/21/2008
5. Formulate a research proposal for the purpose of comparing two methods of implementing new employee orientation.	A. Mendel, RN, D.Ed; S. Sanders, RN, MEd.	11/15/2008

The mission, vision, values, and goal statements are the foundations of your staff development department's practice. As you think about your own statements, consider the trends that currently, or will in the future, affect how your department functions.

References

1. About.com: Human Resources. 2007. *Build a strategic framework: Mission statement, vision, values.* Retrieved February 21, 2008, from *http://humanresources.about.com/cs/strategicplanning1/a/strategicplan_2.htm*.

2. About.com: Human Resources. 2007. *How to implement strategic planning: Vision statement, mission statement, values.* Retrieved February 21, 2008, from *http://humanresources.about.com/od/strategicplannin1/a/implement_plan.htm*.

3. Avillion, A. 2007. *Evidence-Based Staff Development: Strategies to Create, Measure, and Refine your Program.* Marblehead, MA: HCPro, Inc.

4. Avillion, A. 2003. *Writing a Staff Development Plan: Business Strategies for the 21st Century.* Pensacola, FL: The National Nursing Staff Development Organization (NNSDO).

5. Brunt, B. 2001. "Philosophy, mission, and goals." In A. Avillion (Ed.), *Core Curriculum for Staff Development.* 2nd ed. Pensacola, FL: NNSDO. 19–30.

6. Phillips, J., and Phillips, P. 2002. "Reasons why training and development fails and what you can do about it." *Training* 39(9): 78–85.

7. Tiffany, P., and Peterson, S. 1997. *Business Plans for Dummies.* Foster City, CA: IDG Books.

Chapter 3
Healthcare trends and their effect on staff development

Learning Objectives

After reading this chapter, the participant will be able to:

- Discuss the impact of current healthcare trends on staff development
- Describe the facets of an organizational culture of learning

Education is one of the most effective tools for performance improvement and helping staff to deal with the constantly changing healthcare environment. Consider these trends and their effect on staff development practice.

The Impact of Trends

Healthcare trends affect staff development practice by influencing the way patient care is delivered, who delivers that care, and what continuing education and training is necessary to resolve issues that result from these trends. Staff development specialists design their products and services based on needs triggered by changes in the healthcare environment. We must anticipate these needs by analyzing and responding to fluctuations in the healthcare arena.

Maturing of the RN work force is an evolving issue

According to the 2004 National Sample Survey of registered nurses, the average age of RNs was 46.8 years—the highest average age since the first comparable report done in 1980. Only 8% of RNs were younger than 30 years of age and slightly more than 41% were 50 years of age or older (Health Resources and Services Administration 2004).

Program planning and development must take into account the needs of this population. For example, presbyopia, or the progressively reduced capacity to focus on near objects with age, affects many in the RN population. Thus the size of the fonts used in handouts and on computer screens (when using computer-based learning [CBL]) should be at least 12. Be aware of the use of color in handouts and in PowerPoint presentations. Blue and black backgrounds with light-colored lettering provide good visualization.

In an older population, the ability to distinguish high-pitched sounds may also be problematic. Consider lowering the pitch (not volume) of the voice in classroom settings and in the audio component of distance-learning materials. Also consider including assessment of and training in speech and diction when orienting new staff development specialists and other staff who deliver training and continuing education. The ability to clearly and distinctly project one's voice is very important.

Additionally, ergonomics are becoming increasingly important. As we age, joint flexibility may deteriorate. Sitting or standing for long periods of time during education activities may be difficult.

Use your knowledge of age-specific characteristics and incorporate them as part of your program planning and delivery. Evaluate your current programs for age-related appropriateness.

Staffing shortages necessitate new ways of looking at recruitment and retention

Staffing shortages will continue to occur in the healthcare sector. One of the keys to successful recruitment and retention is to avoid knee-jerk responses (e.g., excessive sign-on bonuses) in attempting to deal with such shortages. Why wait until staffing is a critical problem? An organized, ongoing process of recruitment and retention avoids much of the crises associated with these types of problems.

Staff development specialists are critical to developing effective recruitment and retention strategies. Unfortunately, sometimes this participation is limited to planning Nurse Week activities, helping to select the Employee of the Month, and possibly assisting in interviewing potential new employees.

However, implementing strategies such as the following are a more effective use of staff development expertise (Avillion 2005):

- **Educate staff regarding the effective assimilation of new employees.** All too often we hear horror stories of new nurses being treated so shabbily that they resign during or shortly after orientation. Do nurses realize the effect they can have on their new colleagues? Help them to help others by educating them in the art of welcoming and assisting new employees as they enter the organization.

- **Design or update preceptor and mentor programs.** These types of programs are frequently cited as effective recruitment and retention tools.

- **Design and implement interview training.** Nurse managers often expect their clinical leaders to take an active part in recruiting, including interviewing prospective nurses. Have these nurses been trained to effectively participate in the interview process? They need to be.

- **Make orientation as efficient and streamlined as possible.** Assign responsibility for orientation to specific staff development specialists. This includes authority as well as responsibility and allows for consistency in evaluation and implementation. Also, incorporate competency assessment into orientation as much as possible. If pre- and posttests and skill demonstrations are part of competency, include orientees as part of the competency process. Don't waste time setting up separate orientee programs. Establish effective training programs for preceptors and mentors, since, as previously mentioned, effective preceptor and mentor programs are associated with positive recruitment and retention efforts.

Evidence-based practice in staff development will become the norm rather than the exception

Staff educators should not underestimate the importance of implementing evidence-based practice (EBP) in their department. The ultimate goal of EBP in staff development is to provide high-quality, cost-effective education services that are evidence-based (Avillion 2007). EBP in staff development:

- Enables staff development specialists to apply best practices and pertinent research findings to their endeavors

- Supports the need for and stimulates interest in the research process

- Facilitates improvement in job performance and, ultimately, enhances patient outcomes

- Improves communication between the staff development department and other departments by helping to relay the effectiveness of learning activities and justify specific educational approaches

- Increases the job satisfaction of staff development specialists by instituting stimulating endeavors that both justify and improve staff development practice

Continuing education requirements will increase as part of the conditions for licensure, certification, and accreditation achievement

More and more states are requiring that nurses obtain a minimum number of continuing education hours to renew their licenses. Such requirements also exist for renewal of specialty certifications. Additionally, the continuing education of nurses and other healthcare professionals is carefully scrutinized by accrediting organizations such as The Joint Commission and plays a part in prestigious designations.

Staff development departments are expected to facilitate the achievement of continuing education requirements by offering flexible, accessible, and effective training and continuing education.

The need for blended learning will continue to increase

Blended learning, or the use of a variety of education strategies, will continue to increase in importance. Staff development specialists are therefore expected to:

- Identify the most cost-effective, efficient, and flexible means of delivering training and continuing education that positively affects organizational effectiveness

- Facilitate the success of distance learning by ensuring that staff members are able to use the various technologies required for participation in distance learning

- Evaluate blended learning effectiveness objectively by collecting data that provides evidence of education's impact on organizational performance

The cultural and ethnic diversity of patient and employee populations will continue to increase

Staff development specialists are expected to offer training and continuing education in diversity, which is important for the recruitment and retention of employees as well as the welfare of patients. Many staff development departments offer culture-specific classes and training in various languages so that staff members can communicate with patients who do not speak English.

But how many of you offer classes on American culture and English for healthcare professionals who come to the United States and whose native language is not English? It is just as important to help these employees understand American culture—including patient communication—and to help them to acquire skills in the English language.

Generations X and Y (Generation Net) will assume leadership positions as Baby Boomers retire

The first group of Baby Boomers turns 65 years old in 2011. As this generation leaves the workplace, succeeding generations will assume vacated leadership and management positions. This necessitates ongoing management and leadership training, a priority for staff development specialists. Generations X and Y will also need education and training pertaining to:

- Recognition of generational characteristics of those remaining in the workplace

- Anticipation of the characteristics of the generation that will follow theirs in the workplace

- Effective implementation of the "human touch" in the workplace—these generations are accustomed to cyberspace, text messaging, and using technology to communicate and thus sometimes lack the person-to-person skills so important to patient care

The need for business training will increase as the cost of healthcare delivery comes under ever-increasing scrutiny

Education products and services must be aligned with your organization's business strategy. Your ability to objectively document staff development's effect on the organization's financial stability is critical. Because all departments must be able to document such impact, education pertaining to business strategies and financial issues will continue to be a high priority for your department.

Healthcare professionals will need to acquire knowledge and skills at an ever-increasing pace

Rapid advances in technology and the prevention, diagnosis, and treatment of injury and illness require almost daily updates and extensive continuing education. With the retirement of the Baby Boomer generation, orientation of new healthcare employees must be conducted at frequent, time-efficient intervals. This means that accelerated teaching/learning will be an essential staff development technique in the 21st century.

The ability to teach creatively while enhancing learning at a rapid rate is the crux of accelerated learning. Its foundation is the same as adult learning—teaching and learning activities are viewed as dynamic, interactive collaborations with an emphasis on activity-centered learning.

An Organizational Culture of Learning

Organizations are beginning to understand the value of establishing a culture of learning. An organization that supports a culture of learning believes that education is essential for the professional development of all employees and for the continued improvement of patient care services. There is an atmosphere of internal trust among administration, management, and staff that encourages open sharing of knowledge and skills. Integral to the philosophy, values, mission, and vision is a strong belief that education, learning, and knowledge management are essential components of organizational effectiveness.

Organizational leaders are visionaries and use knowledge, learning, and education to facilitate organizational growth. Also, within this culture, senior administration and middle management:

- Highly value and are extremely supportive of education

- Respect those responsible for the coordination and delivery of education products and services

- Facilitate employees' participation in learning activities

- Are responsive to employees' concerns and value their input in decision-making processes

All employees of the organization:

- Know that they are responsible for their own continuing education and professional development and seek out learning activities at every available opportunity

- Support the evaluation of learning activities

- Embrace change and are able to adapt to emerging patient and employee needs

References

1. Avillion, A. 2005. *Nurse Educator Manual: Essential Skills and Guidelines for Effective Practice*. Marblehead, MA: HCPro.

2. Avillion, A. 2007. *Evidence-Based Staff Development: Strategies to Create, Measure, and Refine your Program*. Marblehead, MA: HCPro.

3. Health Resources and Services Administration. 2004. *The registered nurse population: findings from the 2004 National Sample Survey of Registered Nurses*. Retrieved February 17, 2008, from *http://bhpr.hrsa.gov/ healthworkforce/rnsurvey04*.

Chapter 4

Qualifications for the staff development specialist

Learning Objectives

After reading this chapter, the participant will be able to:

- Determine the appropriate qualifications for staff development specialists in an organization
- Identify staff development specialist competencies

Staff development specialists have a great deal of responsibility and must be highly skilled educators and leaders. The ideal candidate has a graduate degree in the adult education field and experience as an educator in the healthcare arena.

However, education and experience are not the only essentials when identifying potential staff development specialists. You are also looking for someone who is a good fit for you, your department, and your organization. The best candidate is one who supports the organizational mission, vision, and values as well as a culture of learning.

To aid the decision-making process, ask candidates to develop and carry out an adult education program for some of your organization's employees. Keep it simple—you don't want them to spend too much time and effort working on a project and then not hire them. Select a learning activity that is relatively easy to implement and give them some guidance about why this program is important to the organization. This will give you an opportunity to observe their program-planning skills and teaching abilities. Ask them to present a proposal for evaluating the effectiveness of their programs as well.

If your department is decentralized, you may have unit- or department-specific educators who are members of the staff development department. Potential clinical and nonclinical educators should demonstrate expertise in their fields and leadership qualities. They should also have a talent for, and interest in, the education process. In conjunction with department managers, you can groom potential educators. Help them develop adult-education, program-planning, and teaching skills and train them in the evaluation process. Consider offering learning activities that deal with teaching skills and education planning. Most clinical employees are responsible for some aspect of patient education and would benefit from such learning activities even if they never want to become educators. You may recognize potential educators during such programs and then determine their interest in educator roles.

You may not have an abundance of experienced staff development specialists as candidates to fill vacancies in your department. So when filling staff development positions, consider hiring people from within the organization. Such candidates may not have experience as staff development specialists, but they do have the advantage of already being part of the culture of the organization. Here are some tips to help you recognize good staff development specialist candidates:

- **Determine basic education requirements.** A background, or the pursuit of a background, in adult education is essential. Make this a requirement. If you want to groom someone without this background, require that he or she achieve either a degree or certificate in adult education within a specified time period and that the person demonstrate his or her active pursuit of this goal regularly.

- **Recognize potential educator talent.** Who has demonstrated indicators such as effective patient education skills or an ability to help peers acquire knowledge? Remember that expertise in a noneducator role does not mean that someone will automatically be a good teacher. The most experienced, excellent staff nurse may not be the best staff development candidate. Effective teaching is an art and a talent.

- **Observe and assess candidates in action.** Interested candidates should plan and carry out an education program with your assistance. They need more help than a staff development candidate with educator experience. This gives you an opportunity not only to observe their education skills, but also to assess how eager they are to pursue the staff development role.

Orientation and Competency

Sometimes experienced staff development specialists forget that they must provide a thorough, competency-based orientation for those new to the staff development specialty. Competencies for staff development specialists are as important as competencies for clinical staff.

Remember that, depending on employees' level of experience, some staff development specialists may be able to successfully challenge orientation components by demonstrating competency in specific areas. Consider including these competencies as not only components of your orientation program, but also as part of your overall competency program for staff development specialists (Avillion 2005, Brunt 2007).

Figure 4.1 on the CD-ROM offers examples of sample competencies for staff development specialists. You may want to adapt and expand upon these ideas. These competencies are not all-inclusive. You will certainly identify more topics for orientation of staff development specialists, as well as additional overall competencies. Use these recommendations as a basis for establishing your own programs.

Writing a Job Description

The qualifications necessary for being a staff educator depend on the roles and responsibilities of the department. Look at your organization's mission, vision, and values. Where does education fit into the organizational plan? Before you determine qualifications and subsequent job descriptions, answer the following questions:

- Do you work in a single hospital or a system that consists of several hospitals or healthcare facilities (e.g., long-term care, hospice, outpatient clinics)?

- If you work in a healthcare system, who is responsible for educational activities? Does this person function at the middle management level or the executive level? To whom does this person report?

- If you work in a single community hospital, who is responsible for staff development? Is this person a middle manager? To whom does this person report?

- Does the staff development department consist of both full- and part-time staff?

- Is the staff development department centralized or decentralized?

- Is the staff development department responsible only for nursing education activities, the entire hospital or health system, or a few specific departments? Who are your primary customers?

- Do some staff members function in dual roles of staff development specialist and direct patient care provider?

- What value does the organization place on education? How does the organization express this in its mission, vision, and values statements?

There are countless ways to determine staff development qualifications because there are countless ways to craft the various roles and responsibilities. Qualifications are and must remain essential components of job descriptions. Following are some guidelines to follow when determining qualifications and translating them into appropriate job descriptions.

Job title

The job title should reflect the position's scope of responsibility. For example, "vice president for education" may be an appropriate title for someone in charge of education for a large health system. But if you are responsible for education services for a large nursing department, "director of staff development for nursing services" may best reflect your role.

Qualifications

Graduate education is the norm for persons holding responsibility for large, systemwide departments. Some large health systems look for doctorally prepared candidates for vice president or director positions. Many healthcare organizations expect all staff development specialists to be prepared at the master's level. Explicit education qualifications will depend on specific roles and responsibilities. For example, a vice president for education or director of staff development needs managerial qualifications, including business expertise, in addition to qualifications in education. Clinical expertise is not essential. In fact, clinical staff development specialists may find themselves reporting to someone who has graduate degrees in business or education, but no clinical background.

Be specific about length and type of experience needed, put it in writing, and stick to it. A director role may require experience as a middle manager in addition to education experience. An information systems trainer needs specific expertise as a computer specialist. Make sure that experience requirements correlate with job responsibilities.

If you find an ideal candidate who is currently working on a required graduate degree, you may decide to allow that person a specific amount of time to complete his or her education. However, be explicit about the time frame in which the degree must be earned and put it in writing. Be sure that the employee understands the consequences of failing to earn this degree. These consequences should also be in writing.

General working conditions

Be as specific as possible about the hours required, including the need to work weekends, holidays, and shift work as appropriate. This is especially true if you are sharing a position with another department (e.g., an RN working as a clinical educator for the staff development department 24 hours per week and as a bedside nurse 16 hours per week).

Identify any physical demands, such as, "Must be able to lift, move, and position equipment including classroom chairs, tables, and audiovisual equipment of at least 30 pounds regularly." Also identify any potential for exposure to dangerous situations, such as dealing with patients who have infectious diseases or are violent. List the observance of specific precautions (e.g., mandatory training on dealing with violence, wearing protective clothing, etc.).

Reporting mechanism

Clearly define reporting lines. If someone reports to two managers, as in the case of a shared position, make sure the reporting structure is made clear.

Summary of responsibilities

This general summary should include an overview of responsibilities, including what positions, if any, this particular position supervises. It should also include a statement about ensuring that services are consistent with the organizational and departmental mission, vision, values, and goals.

Major responsibilities

Identify major responsibilities as competency statements with qualifiers. Refer back to Figure 4.1 for examples of such responsibilities phrased in terms of competency. You should also include responsibilities as they pertain to EBP in staff development. Here are some examples:

- Gathers and analyzes data to use as evidence for program planning, design, implementation, and evaluation

- Uses evidence obtained via data analysis to identify best practices and benchmarks in staff development

- Uses evidence to identify staff development research topics

- Participates in staff development research

Be sure to note attendance at mandatory education events and how many hours of continuing education should be attained every year. Also, include a statement explaining that responsibilities will be assessed and modified on an ongoing basis in accordance with the needs of the organization.

References

1. Avillion, A. 2005. *Nurse Educator Manual: Essential Skills and Guidelines for Effective Practice*. Marblehead, MA: HCPro.

2. Brunt, B. 2007. *Competencies for Staff Educators: Tools to Evaluate and Enhance Nursing Professional Development*. Marblehead, MA: HCPro.

Chapter 5

Evolving roles of the staff development specialist

The Many Hats of the Staff Development Specialist

Staff development specialists fulfill multiple roles. The responsibilities for education are clear cut. But are you prepared to assume one or more of the roles that have recently found their way into the staff development arena? To help you determine your preparedness, read the following descriptions of some of these new roles and the issues that accompany them.

CLO or CKO

The chief learning officer (CLO) or chief knowledge officer (CKO) is the person responsible for discerning, organizing, and documenting the collective knowledge of a healthcare organization. The CLO has the opportunity to significantly influence the evolution of the organization. This person oversees the provision of education endeavors for the organization and is instrumental in evaluating the impact of knowledge, learning, and education in the organization.

The CLO or CKO is typically a member of the senior administrative team and fulfills a strategic role. This is a new role, and to justify its existence, education's positive effect on the organization—including its financial solvency—must be objectively demonstrated (Donner 2000, Stuller 1998).

Director of the center for excellence

Similar to the roles of the CLO or CKO, the director of the center for excellence emphasizes the educational goal of achieving excellence among an organization's employees, patients, and products and services. The director is expected to associate the education and professional development of employees with excellence in patient care and organizational effectiveness. He or she is expected to furnish evidence of this association.

Manager

The manager for a staff development department is responsible for guiding staff development activities, including overseeing program development, evaluation, and performance of his or her staff (Fischer et al 2001). The manager must also possess managerial skills, including:

* Human resource management
* Knowledge of and adherence to labor relations mandates
* Budgetary management
* Acting in a leadership model capacity

Performance coach

The ability to enhance job performance is frequently viewed as part of the educator's role. A performance coach functions as just that—a coach, role model, and talent developer.

Coaching may be done one on one or in a group. You may be asked to coach staff, managers, physicians, administrators or any member of the organization. This role requires a great deal of tact and political savvy (Churley-Strom et al 2001).

Consultant

Staff development specialists have informally acted as consultants for many years. Recently, however, the role has become more formal. Consultations are sought in many areas, such as performance improvement, skill attainment, leadership development, and preparation for accreditation surveys. This facet of the staff development role requires expertise in the subject matter and excellent interpersonal skills (Wright et al 2001).

Researcher

Participation in clinical and quality improvement research is often part of the staff development specialist's role. In some health systems, nursing research falls in the realm of education services. This is most often the case in large health systems where the department director has a doctorate. The staff development specialist as researcher is expected to identify and participate in research to:

- Improve patient outcomes
- Add to the body of knowledge unique to staff development practice
- Research to enhance organizational effectiveness

Clinical research findings enhance education program development. Learners acquire new knowledge and skills that, when applied, improve patient outcomes (Schoenly 2001).

However, clinical researcher is not the only research role a staff development specialist may assume. He or she is also responsible for conducting and analyzing research findings from staff development studies. The research component of staff development is important to evidence-based practice (EBP). The basis of EBP in staff development includes the findings from staff development research. Benchmarks and best practices from such research are incorporated into staff development practice.

OD specialist

Organizational development (OD) focuses on providing a framework to manage an organization as a smoothly functioning system. The OD specialist's primary function is to facilitate organization-wide change while enhancing working relationships and performance improvement. These duties come naturally to the staff development role because, traditionally, educators work to improve work performance and facilitate the achievement of organizational goals (Ritt 2001).

Roles and responsibilities will continue to evolve and expand in scope and importance to the organization. Be on the alert for healthcare conditions that could trigger new roles and duties. As these roles evolve, consider what qualifications are needed to fulfill them.

References

1. Churley-Strom, R., and McCarthy, M. 2001. "Role of the performance coach in staff development." In A. Avillion (Ed.) *Core curriculum for staff development*. 2nd ed. Pensacola, FL: The National Nursing Staff Development Organization (NNSDO). 561–578.

2. Donner, D. 2000. "Four facts about the new jobs of chief learning officer and chief knowledge officer." *Performance in Practice* (supplement to *Training & Development Magazine*). Fall 2000: 1–2.

3. Fischer, K., Franck, L, and Seay, S. 2001. "Role of the manager in staff development." In A. Avillion (Ed.) *Core Curriculum for Staff Development*. 2nd ed. Pensacola, FL: The National Nursing Staff Development Organization (NNSDO). 483–512.

4. Ritt, E. 2001. "Role of the organization development specialist in staff development." In A. Avillion (Ed.) *Core Curriculum for Staff Development*. 2nd ed. Pensacola, FL: The National Nursing Staff Development Organization (NNSDO). 535–548.

5. Schoenly, L., and Pillar, B. 2001. "Role of the researcher in staff development." In A. Avillion (ed.) *Core Curriculum for Staff Development*. 2nd ed. Pensacola, FL: The National Nursing Staff Development Organization (NNSDO). 523–534.

6. Stuller, J. 1998. "Chief of corporate smarts." *Training*. 35(4): 28–34.

7. Wright, D., and Woodward, T. 2001. "Role of the consultant in staff development." In A. Avillion (ed.) *Core Curriculum for Staff Development*. 2nd ed. Pensacola, FL: The National Nursing Staff Development Organization (NNSDO). 513–522.

Unit 2

Teaching Adults

Chapter 6
Principles of adult learning

Learning Objectives

After reading this chapter, the participant will be able to:

- Implement the principles of adult learning in all education activities

Nearly all staff development specialist job descriptions include a statement about the "implementation of adult learning principles." However, when it comes to applying these principles, organizations sometimes merely give them lip service.

Adult learning principles must be actively implemented to deliver quality adult education. These principles are also important when gathering data that serve as a foundation for evidence-based staff development practice. This chapter reviews the principles of adult learning and offers recommendations for their practical implementation.

The Principles

The principles of adult learning are more than rules or guidelines; they form the foundation of the adult learner's reasons for partaking and interest in lifelong learning. Staff development specialists must implement them in ways that that enhance education and motivate adults in their educational pursuits.

Adults need a reason for learning

Developing clear-cut objectives for an educational program, although always important, is not enough.

Adult learners want to know why it is important to participate in an educational activity (Bland et al 2001). For example, suppose you have been told to implement organizationwide customer-service training. Some staff may respond by complaining, "I already know how to talk to patients. This is just a waste of time." However, staff members may feel differently if they know that quality improvement data indicate a trend in customer dissatisfaction. They need to know what complaints and concerns patients and other customers express and why it is important to address them. Staff members also need to know that customer satisfaction is the responsibility of all employees.

The necessity of motivating your learners shows the need for evidence-based practice in staff development. If you gather evidence that links education to positive patient or organizational outcomes, you are better able to justify education and motivate learners.

Communicating facts relevant to the rationale for a particular program is essential. Adults have the right and the responsibility to know why they are asked to acquire or maintain knowledge and skills.

Adults are self-directed learners

Adult learners direct and are responsible for their own learning. They need to have some control over what they learn and how they learn it. Adults also need to feel that their learning needs are respected (Bland et al 2001, Merriam et al 1997).

Although some training is not learner-directed (e.g., classes mandated by The Joint Commission), it is possible to offer learners choices about how they will learn the material.

Suppose the safe administration of chemotherapy is an essential competency for oncology nurses as well as a component of orientation for newly hired oncology nurses.
Offer two teaching methods:

- **A self-learning module.** If successfully completed, this method allows those nurses to be exempt from the formal classroom or computer-based learning settings.

- **Demonstration of safe administration.** This may be part of a skills laboratory for nurses who have little or no experience in this field. But experienced nurses who successfully complete the didactic self-learning component and demonstrate safe administration in the work setting may be exempted from this type of demonstration. This approach allows self-direction and acknowledges existing expertise.

Adults bring a variety of life experiences to any learning situation

Life experiences enhance any learning situation (Bland et al 2001, Merriam et al 1997). Such experiences may not directly relate to the specific topic of the program, but they can still complement learning. If you teach a program about customer service in healthcare, participants may relate stories about their own experiences in various settings from the perspective of the customer rather than the provider of services. Encourage the sharing of relevant experiences, but do not allow any one participant to dominate the discussion.

Adults focus on acquiring knowledge and skills that will help them improve their daily lives

Adults need to understand how particular knowledge and skills will benefit them as they conduct their daily activities. These benefits can be related to work or their personal lives. In other words, adults are task-, problem-, or life-centered in their approach to learning.

This correlates well with adults' need to know. You can help by including a practical rationale, based on evidence gathered from sources such as program evaluations, risk management data, and performance evaluations, for learning activities and making objectives clear and measurable.

Adults are responsive to both extrinsic and intrinsic motivators

Extrinsic motivators include such factors as promotions, salary increases, better jobs, and better working conditions. Intrinsic motivators include improved quality of life, enhanced job satisfaction, and increased self-esteem (Merriam et al 1997). Adults need to know that the knowledge and skills obtained from an activity will satisfy their extrinsic and intrinsic needs.

Figure 6.1 on the CD-ROM is a template that will help you use adult learning principles during the program planning process. It identifies specific adult learning principles and important components of each and provides space for you to customize your learning activities.

References

1. Bland, G., and Hadaway, L. 2001. "Principles of adult learning," *Core Curriculum for Staff Development*. 2nd ed. Pensacola, FL: The National Nursing Staff Development Organization (NNSDO). 31–64.

2. Merriam, S., and Brockett, R. 1997. *The Profession and Practice of Adult Education: An Introduction*. San Francisco, CA: Jossey-Bass.

Chapter 7
Identifying learning styles

Learning Objectives

After reading this chapter, the participant will be able to:

- Describe characteristics of various learning styles
- Identify teaching strategies associated with various learning styles

It is not enough to understand and use the principles of adult learning. You must also consider various learning styles, generational differences, and cultural influences that affect how your audience retains information. This chapter deals with learning styles and how these styles influence ability to learn.

Some learners may not be aware of their learning styles. Help your learners recognize their learning preferences and design programs that match teaching strategies to learning styles.

The Learning Styles

Most experts recognize three distinct styles of learning: auditory, visual, and kinesthetic. However, some researchers divide these styles into subgroups for even more clarification. The following descriptions include the characteristics of each style, learner behaviors, and what you can do to accommodate learners of all three styles.

Auditory

Auditory learners learn predominantly by hearing. These learners prefer audiotapes, lectures, and discussions and respond best to verbal instructions. Their preference for auditory learning is evident even in their everyday speech, as they frequently make comments like, "I hear what you're saying," "I'm telling myself," and "That sounds good to me." Auditory learners often read out loud. As they speak, their brains are stimulated to assimilate knowledge and skills (Miller 2000).

Your auditory learners will position themselves in a classroom or other learning environment so they can hear, but they don't necessarily need to have the best view of the educator. They do not enjoy written handouts or visuals. This can be a particular challenge during distance-learning activities, such as computer-based learning (CBL). If possible, add auditory stimulants (e.g., verbal conversations or music) to the program.

Here are some facets of the auditory learning experience and suggestions for meeting these learners' needs. Auditory learners:

- Reveal their emotions through changes in their tone of voice and the quality of their speech. Assess their satisfaction with the learning experience by listening to how they express themselves. They may say everything is fine, but their tone of voice tells you the opposite is true.
- Give excellent verbal directions and explanations.
- Talk aloud through problems and procedures and expresses solutions verbally.
- Benefit from verbally recording study notes and listening to them instead of reading them when studying.

Aural (auditory-musical-rhythmic) learners

This style of learner has many of the characteristics of the auditory learner, with some qualifications. Like auditory learners, aural learners respond to sound. But they like to involve sound and music as part of the learning process, have a good sense of rhythm, and can sing or play musical instruments. They uses phrases such as, "That rings a bell," "Tune in to these instructions," and "This is as clear as a bell."

Aural learners study best when they hear music in the background. Memory is enhanced when topics or information are associated with specific songs or sounds (Learning-styles-online.com 2007 *The aural [auditory-musical-rhythmic] learning style*).

Visual learners

During adulthood, visual learning is the predominant learning style. Visual learners prefer to sit at the front of the classroom, take copious notes, and are attracted to verbal discussions that contain a lot of imagery.

These learners prefer passive surroundings and are attracted to presentations and handouts that use color, graphics, and other visual stimuli. They tend to be distracted by too much auditory stimulation. Visual learners may close their eyes to visualize what they're learning (Miller 2000). When working with visual learners, ensure that:

- Handouts are well-illustrated and colorful

- The educator is easily seen in the classroom setting

- Written materials are easy to read (i.e., avoid small print)

Visual/spatial learners

Visual/spatial learners prefer the use of images, pictures, colors, and maps when communicating and organizing information. These learners have a good sense of direction and rely on visualization to solve problems. Visual/spatial learners use phrases such as "I can picture this in my mind," "I'd like to use a diagram," and "I need a different perspective on this problem."

Color, layout, and spatial organization are important. Consider this when designing handouts, visuals, and CBL. Graphs, diagrams, and maps are all useful teaching tools (Learning-styles-online. com 2007 *The visual [spatial] learning style*).

Verbal (linguistic) learners

Verbal learners depend on both the written and spoken word and effectively express themselves both verbally and in writing. They enjoy learning new words and using the meanings of these words in conversations and written projects. Verbal learners thrive during debates and when expressing their viewpoints in writing. They use phrases such as, "Let me spell this out for you," and "Let me explain this word for word."

Verbal learners talk themselves through procedures and use rhyme and rhythm in memorization. Like auditory learners, verbal learners benefit from recording important facts and memorize by listening to audiotapes (Learning-styles-online.com 2007 *The verbal [linguistic] learning style*).

Kinesthetic learners

Kinesthetic learners learn by physical activities and direct hands-on involvement. These people learn best by doing (Miller 2000). They use their bodies and sense of touch to learn about their environments. Kinesthetic learners are sensitive to textures. They work through problems during physical activities like jogging.

Kinesthetic learners need activity and cannot sit still for long periods of time, and thus need frequent breaks. These learners speak with their hands and display emotions through body language. They may remember what activities were performed during a training exercise but have trouble remembering what they saw or what was said (Learning-styles-online.com 2007 *The physical [bodily-kinesthetic] learning style*). These learners frequently use phrases such as, "Keep in touch," "I can't grasp this information," and "I'm following your directions." Here are suggestions for working with kinesthetic learners:

- Provide opportunities for skill demonstrations and return demonstrations.

- When directions are given, use demonstration whenever possible. This can be done in person, on videos, or during CBL.

- Provide opportunities for these learners to get up and move around.

 Use Figure 7.1 on the CD-ROM to plan educational activities that include techniques suitable for all learners.

Right- and Left-Brain Learner Characteristics

The right and left hemispheres of the brain process information differently. These differences influence how we learn (About.com 2007, Forrest 2004). The left side of the brain processes information from the parts to the whole in a logical, linear manner. The right brain processes information holistically, focusing on the big picture and then breaking it down to its subsequent parts. The right brain emphasizes the visual, while the left brain is verbal.

Left-brain learners value an orderly sequence of events. They often make lists and deal effectively with symbols, mathematics, words, and letters. Left-brain learners excel at sequencing tasks, such as spelling. They are logical and gather data piece by piece to make conclusions and decisions. They are also articulate, expressive speakers.

Right-brain learners process information randomly, moving from task to task without planning and without setting priorities. They dislike study schedules or planning their days too rigidly. Sensitive to color, right-brain learners often find it helpful to organize materials by color using stickers, Post-it notes, or visual illustrations. They are intuitive and follow their instincts but have difficulty expressing themselves articulately. Although they may know the answers to test questions or verbal discussion questions, they have trouble finding the right words to express themselves (Middle Tennessee State University 2006).

Figure 7.2 describes the characteristics of right- and left-brain learners and teaching strategies to nurture both preferences.

Figure 7.2

Left-brain learners vs. right-brain learners

Hemisphere Preference	Characteristics	Teaching Strategies
Left-brain learners	• Process information from its parts to the whole in a logical, linear manner • Emphasize the verbal • Value an orderly sequence of events • Make lists and check off tasks as they are accomplished • Learn information easily through sequencing (such as spelling) • Deal effectively with symbols, mathematics, words, and letters • Articulate and excel at verbal presentations	Offer learning activities that include verbal discussions, debates, and presentations. Conduct learning activities in an organized manner with an obvious beginning and conclusion. Facilitate learning by associating concepts with symbols and specific word sequences.
Right-brain learners	• Process information holistically, focusing on the big picture and then breaking it down to its subsequent parts • Emphasize the visual • Process information randomly, going from one task to another without setting priorities • Dislike schedules • Are sensitive to color • Follows instincts and intuition • Prefer things to be concrete and likes to be able to see, hear, or touch an actual object	Organize tasks through the use of color and visuals. For example, use various color coded stickers to help with organization skills and note taking. Offer learning activities that can be accessed in a flexible manner, without requiring adherence to rigid time frames. Illustrate notes or other written materials with concrete examples of conceptual ideas.

References

1. About.com. (2007). *Right brain and left brain inventory.* Retrieved March 10, 2008, from *http://painting.about.com/library/blpain/blrightbraintable.htm.*

2. Forrest, S. 2004. "Learning and teaching: The reciprocal link." *The Journal of Continuing Education in Nursing* 35(2): 74–79.

3. Learning-styles-online.com. 2007. *The aural (auditory-musical-rhythmic) learning style.* Retrieved March 10, 2008, from *www.learning-styles-online.com/style/aural-auditory-musical.*

4. Learning-styles-online.com. 2007. *The physical (bodily-kinesthetic) learning style.* Retrieved March 10, 2008, from *www.learning-styles-online.com/style/visual-spatial.*

5. Learning-styles-online.com. 2007. *The verbal (linguistic) learning style.* Retrieved March 10, 2008, from *www.learning-styles-online.com/style/verbal-linguistic.*

6. Learning-styles-online.com. 2007. *The visual (spatial) learning style.* Retrieved March 10, 2008, from *www.learning-styles-online.com/style/visual-spatial.*

7. Middle Tennessee State University. 2006. *Left vs. right: Which side are you on?* Retrieved August 7, 2006, from *www.mtsu.edu/~studskl/hd/learn.*

8. Miller, S. 2000. *Three different learning styles.* Retrieved April 28, 2003, from *www.usd.edu/trio/tut/ts/styleres.html.*

Chapter 8
Teaching multigenerational audiences

Are there really differences in learning preferences among various generations? The answer is a resounding "yes." Of course, no one style or preference is common to all members of a specific generation. But a learner's generation is one of many factors to consider when planning education activities. This chapter describes general guidelines to help you teach multigenerational audiences more effectively.

The current work force is composed of four specific generations: Veterans, Baby Boomers, Generation X, and Generation Y. The following descriptions identify each generation's view of the world, their beliefs about what constitutes an appealing work environment, and their preferences for how they acquire knowledge and skills. Finally, sample templates to help you plan programs for multigenerational audiences are offered.

Veterans

The generation born between 1926 and 1945 experienced firsthand two of the most critical events of the 20th century: the Great Depression and World War II. Therefore, Veterans possess experiences unique to those events, as the events shaped how they view themselves and the world in which they live (Hammill 2005, Filipczak et al 1999).

Veterans' view of family is that of a traditional nuclear family, consisting of two parents and their children within one household. They value education, considering it a dream to work toward. They believe in paying cash for purchases and dislike debt.

Members of this generation have the most vivid memories of parents and grandparents who came as immigrants to the United States. They possess knowledge of cultural traditions, wisdom, and wit that succeeding generations generally lack. They believe in hard work and adherence to rules.

Often, Veterans prefer more formal learning environments and dislike being asked to relay or listen to stories or experiences they deem too personal. They believe that educational experiences should be more formal; as learners, they expect educators to be well-dressed and behave in a businesslike fashion. Profanity and slang should be avoided.

Members of this generation view educators as authority figures to be respected. Therefore, they are the least likely of all learners to confront you directly if they disagree with you. You may not find out they disliked the way an activity was conducted until you read their program evaluations (Hammill 2005).

Teaching considerations

The following are tips for Veterans, but note that some of these points are applicable to any adult learner:

- Make sure learning goals and objectives are clearly understood, regardless of the teaching method used. This is especially important if distance-learning techniques are used.

- When using distance learning, make it clear where these learners should go for help with new or unfamiliar technology. For example, an important part of computer-based learning (CBL) is to include the educator's contact information. Will you be available for face-to-face discussion, or will you work with your learners via e-mail? Let them know when and where you will be available or how soon they can expect a response to an e-mail question.

- Provide organized handouts that summarize key points of the education activity.

- Avoid small print when developing handouts or writing CBL programs. Use a computer font that is easily read, such as Arial, and don't use any font sizes less than a 12.

- Do not put members of this generation on the spot by asking uncomfortable questions or asking them to demonstrate unfamiliar techniques, especially in front of younger colleagues. Encourage participation in a nonthreatening way.

- Treat them with respect at all times.

- Establish rapport, especially if you are a younger educator. Acknowledge their life experiences, wisdom, and expertise.

- Never presume all members of this generation are computer illiterate.

- Never talk down to them.

- Motivate these learners by explaining how education will improve job performance and organizational effectiveness.

- If skill demonstration is part of the activity, allow them time for practice in private.

- Because Veterans are unlikely to confront you in person, encourage feedback during breaks or midway through a distance-learning activity.

Baby Boomers

The Baby Boomers are the product of the post–World War II baby boom. Born between 1946 and 1964, the Boomer generation consists of an estimated 73 million people. Baby Boomers were usually doted on by their parents and grew up believing they were entitled to the best the world had to offer. They also view education as a birthright. In their youth, Boomers believed it was their right and their responsibility to change the world for the better. This generation has a passionate work ethic and a desire to achieve financial success. Baby Boomers coined the phrase "Thank God it's Monday" and the 60-hour work week. They also spend freely, with an attitude of "Buy now, pay later." But Boomers view the Veterans' traditional family unit as disintegrating (Hammill 2005, News Digest 2001 "Baby Boomers," Filipczak et al 1999).

Baby Boomers value both teamwork and personal gratification in the workplace. They are dedicated to learning and initiated the self-help book craze. Boomers don't usually respond well to authority figures: They may come across with an "I already know that" attitude. They respond best to educators who treat them as equals and share personal examples of their own knowledge and skills. Beware of too much familiarity in a multigenerational setting, however. Do not alienate Veterans while accommodating Boomers by relating personal anecdotes.

Teaching considerations

Baby Boomers are motivated to learn if newly acquired knowledge and skills will help them excel on the job and gain recognition. Consider these tips when planning education for Baby Boomers:

- Correlate the educational activities with improved job performance.

- Incorporate interactive educational activities such as icebreakers and discussions.

- Boomers are team-oriented and enjoy team learning activities.

- Avoid role-playing activities; most boomers do not like them.

- Allow time for private practice. Like most adult learners, Boomers don't like to display lack of knowledge or skill in public.

- Use learning activities that provide personal challenges and allow Baby Boomers to use life experiences as part of education.

- Make information easily and readily accessible. Remember, this was the first generation to use the Internet.

Generation X

Generation X, composed of people born between 1965 and 1980, has also been deemed the "latch-key generation." Defining events Generation Xers' lives included Watergate, President Nixon's resignation, the growing trend of single-parent families, and the increasing use of computers as part of everyday life.

Members of Generation X are cautious about money and believe in saving. They view education as a means to achieve success.

In contrast to the Baby Boomers, who often live to work, the Xers work to live and value a reasonable balance between work and personal time. Xers value flexibility, dislike close supervision, and prefer self-directed learning. They are comfortable with change and see it as the norm rather than the exception. Having seen their parents' experience with downsizing, they grew accustomed to changes in their parents' financial status and in family structures. Because of this, Xers are not loyal to a particular organization; they are loyal to themselves (Hammill 2005, News Digest 2001 "Generation Xers," Filipczak et al 1999). Their attitude can be described as, "It's only a job."

Teaching considerations

Be aware that there are distinct differences—even conflicts—between how Boomers and Xers view the world, adopt work ethics, and value education and training. These differences can make it a challenge for them to work together. Generation Xers do not need or want classroom interaction or team activities. They prefer self-directed learning at a time and place convenient for them. They dislike having to be at a specific place at a specific time to participate in learning activities. Xers are born distance learners.

Here are more tips for involving Xers in teaching/learning activities:

- Make learning activities fun. Xers value fun as part of any work or learning activity.

- Include hands-on learning activities and activities in which learners learn by doing. Xers love role-playing scenarios and are not worried about making mistakes in front of others as they learn.

- Allow plenty of time for discussion, especially if you are teaching in a classroom setting. Xers are enthusiastic learners and ask lots of questions. If distance learning is the teaching method, clearly identify how their questions will be answered (e.g., e-mail, face-to-face meetings, etc.).

- Be clear about your availability to answer questions. Xers want educators to be available to answer questions and facilitate learning, but they do not want to feel pressured or crowded. They need their freedom.

- Earn their respect early by demonstrating your expertise and enthusiasm to help them learn. Xers do not automatically respect authority figures, including educators. You need to earn it.

- Include a lot of visual stimulation (e.g., graphics, tables, pictures, etc.). Xers don't read as much as the boomers; they prefer these visual methods over printed narratives.

Generation Y

Generation Y, composed of people born between 1981 and 2002, is also referred to as the Echo-Boom Generation or Generation Net. An estimated 80 million Ys will displace the 77 million Baby Boomers and the 44 million Xers, eventually redefining the workplace.

This generation has grown up in the technological age. The Internet is as commonplace for them as the television was for Boomers. Generation Y grew up with computers, CD players, and VCRs and DVDs. They are comfortable with the tools associated with distance learning.

Often, Ys value diversity. They are highly motivated and understand that knowledge and skills will increase their ability to find good jobs. They are also accustomed to sharing the workload from a young age, as they generally held part-time jobs during high school and college. They view money as an "earn-to-spend" commodity.

Thanks to the Internet and other technological advances, Ys are globally oriented. They know and understand that there is no such thing as geographic isolation or protection, as illustrated to them by 9/11. Their concept of family is different from that of Veterans and Boomers: Single parenthood, same-sex partnerships, and grandparents as primary parent figures are only some of the ways Ys define their families.

Ys have even less company loyalty than Xers do. They have seen downsizing become almost a norm and have witnessed a constant stream of mergers, takeovers, closings, and acquisitions. Company loyalty is not a factor in their career paths; they anticipate numerous job changes as they pursue their careers. The focus of their work life is not on where they work but on what they do. They respect those who demonstrate expertise and knowledge, but they do not necessarily equate these characteristics with age, rank, or tenure (Alch 2000, Hammill 2005, Filipczak et al 1999).

Teaching considerations

Ys thrive best in work environments that offer them a direct say in how the organization functions and encourage their input (Alch 2000, Filipczak et al 1999, Hammill 2005). They want to perform their jobs to the best of their abilities. When planning teaching activities for Ys, think about the following characteristics associated with this generation. Ys:

- Enjoy the opportunity to interact with their colleagues during training
- Have strong work ethics
- Look for structure as well as fun in the workplace and during education activities
- Enjoy entertaining, varied education activities
- Are comfortable with the technology of distance learning but prefer interactive opportunities
- Benefit most from mentor programs

- Are interested in earning a good living and value education that will increase their ability to earn money

- View education as incredibly expensive

- Enjoy creative teaching techniques, including the incorporation of music and games

- Are readers and value the time they spend reading

Multigenerational Education

Because you will be dealing with all four generations, plan varied activities that meet at least some of the needs of each generation. Explain why certain techniques are being used to help learners accept the necessity of being involved in activities that do not meet their personal preferences (e.g., role play for Boomers, strict timetables for Xers).

Figure 8.1 on the CD-ROM included with this book contains a multigenerational teaching techniques organizer that you can customize to ensure that you are implementing teaching methodologies that address every generation in your audience. The chart summarizes the major characteristics of each generation discussed in this chapter. You can use the "Teaching techniques" column to plan specific learning activities that meet the needs of each generation of learners.

References

1. Alch, M. 2000. "Get ready for the Net Generation." *Training* 37(2): 32–33.

2. Filipczak, B., Raines, C., and Zemke, R. 1999. "Generation gaps in the classroom." *Training* 36(11): 48–54.

3. Hammill, G. 2005. Mixing and managing four generations of employees. *FDU Magazine online*, Winter/Spring 2005. Retrieved March 10, 2008, from *www.fdu.edu/newspubs/magazine/05ws/generations.htm*.

4. News Digest. 2001. "Baby boomers." *Training*. Retrieved August 24, 2002, at *www.trainingmag.com*.

5. News Digest. 2001. "Generation Xers." *Training*. Retrieved August 24, 2002, at *www.trainingmag.com*.

Chapter 9
Designing cultural diversity education

Learning Objectives

After reading this chapter, the participant will be able to:

- Identify ways to design effective diversity education

Cultural diversity is a valued component of our society. Staff development specialists teach learners who represent a variety of cultures, so educators must consider what effects culture has on learning.

Healthcare professionals have varied views about what the term *cultural diversity* means and the actual purpose of cultural diversity training. They may believe that such training is initiated primarily to help them avoid professional and legal problems rather than improve patient care (Nisha et al 2007). However, staff development specialists know that the primary purposes of cultural diversity education are to improve:

- Healthcare professional–patient communication
- Healthcare professional–family communication
- Communication among healthcare professionals
- Patient and family outcomes

Cultural diversity education is also a requirement of some accrediting agencies. However, this is not the primary purpose of such education. Your cultural diversity programming should be practical and based on evidence that directs its design.

Here are some recommendations for the design of cultural diversity education:

- Identify the most predominant cultural groups in your patient population

- Identify the most predominant cultural groups in your organization's employee population

- Identify people who are well-versed in these cultures and in the native languages of these cultures to assist with education

- Investigate the feasibility of offering English as a Second Language (ESL) courses in your organization

- Include American cultural characteristics as part of your diversity training

- Prepare written guidelines for dealing with specific critical aspects of persons from cultures most frequently seen in your organization

Realistically, you cannot offer cultural diversity for all cultures represented in your organization's employee and patient populations, so prioritize education needs. Gather data pertaining to cultural background and use this data as evidence to justify your program planning.

For example, suppose you live and work in the Pacific Northwest. A significant number of your patients and colleagues represent Native American and Asian American groups, and many of your patients and colleagues are also natives of Asian countries. Your priority when designing cultural diversity education is based on these cultures. However, that does not mean you can ignore cultural needs of other groups.

 Use Figure 9.1 to develop guidelines for swift, on-demand cultural training needs.

Offer English as a Second Language Training

It may be to your organization's advantage to offer an ESL course for employees. Employees whose native language is not English are at a disadvantage when communicating with their English-speaking colleagues and patients. It is impossible to understand diverse cultures if staff members and patients cannot talk to one another. If there is a predominant cultural population of patients and staff within your organization (e.g., Hispanic or Asian), consider offering a course in that population's native language for your English-speaking staff. Many colleges, universities, and high schools offer this type of course.

You may be able to negotiate having a course brought on site to your organization on a regular basis. A good place to start negotiations is with any colleges or universities that have student affiliations with your organization.

Justify the expense of this type of education using evidence from quality improvement data from patient satisfaction surveys, evaluations from educational programs, adverse occurrence reports related to communicative or cultural differences, performance-evaluation data, and orientation feedback from new employees.

Be sure to measure the impact of your cultural diversity training. The same data used to justify expenses are used to provide evidence that such training has a positive impact on patient outcomes.

Include American Culture as Part of Diversity Education

Although Americans represent a variety of ethnic and racial backgrounds, some cultural distinctions are truly American. For example, most Americans value eye contact as an indicator of attention and concentration. Asian and Middle Eastern cultures avoid eye contact and may consider it insulting or an indication of sexual promiscuity, so, for example, a nurse who has just arrived from Japan or Jordan needs to understand the significance of eye contact to Americans (Galanti 2003, Narayan 2003).

Americans also have a reputation of being loud and boisterous. A nurse colleague related the following experience that took place as she dined in a restaurant with her French husband.

> *"We were in a small restaurant in a Paris suburb, and I overheard the people at the next table speaking English and talking about the upcoming Super Bowl game. I immediately introduced myself as a fellow American and soon we were having an animated conversation about football and where we lived in the United States. After they left the restaurant I noticed that my husband looked rather uncomfortable and embarrassed. I also noticed that other French diners were looking at me. My husband explained that in France, people would never have conversations with strangers simply because they were from the same country. It just isn't done."*

Other American characteristics include placing great value on independence and individual success, as well as having a fierce belief in individual rights and freedom. There are also American characteristics unique to particular areas of the country, including:

- **Terminology.** For example, depending on the area of the country in which you live, the terms *soda, soda pop,* and *pop* all refer to carbonated beverages such as Coca Cola.

- **Pronunciation.** Various regions of the country have particular accents and different ways of pronouncing the same words.

- **Expressions of speech.** For example, suppose you are ordering a particular item at a restaurant only to be told, "It's all." Persons living in south central Pennsylvania understand that this means there is no more of that item. In other words, it's all gone.

- **Food preferences.** Coffee-loving persons of Scandinavian descent in Minnesota can be counted on to always have a pot of coffee brewing. It helps to know what food items hold a particularly important place in certain geographic areas.

Include Cultural Diversity Training in Orientation

It is not easy to add more content to an orientation program. However, cultural awareness will help new employees to assimilate into the organization. Role play, discussion, and distance-learning techniques can all be used to provide basic information. Allow time for in-person discussion as well. Include information about how cultural differences manifest themselves in patients, visitors, and colleagues and present learners with scenarios that require them to make choices based on cultural appropriateness.

What topics should you include as part of diversity education?

It is not possible to include all aspects of multiple cultures in a diversity program. However, if cultural diversity is part of your competency program, you can regularly add material about aspects of various cultures.

The following is information to include in your initial training:

- How do members of this culture communicate? What significance do body language, gestures, tone of voice, and eye contact have? Which family members take the lead in communicating with people outside of their culture?

- What specific family/gender issues exist? What is the woman's role? How are major decisions made?

- What role does religion play?

- How is pain expressed?

- What are common health practices (e.g., alternative medicine, herbal medicine, home remedies, etc.)?

- How do families deal with pregnancy and births?

- Is there a standard work ethic valued in the culture? How are specific occupations viewed in terms of respectability, financial need, and appropriateness?

- Are there dietary restrictions associated with this culture?

- Are there specific political beliefs that influence people of this culture?

- Are there specific conflicts between certain cultural groups that may surface within your organization?

After you have identified the cultures you will include in your diversity education, use Figure 9.1 the Diversity education planner template on the CD-ROM to customize your plan. Enter a culture and organize the important considerations for that culture under each appropriate heading. You can also use this template to develop reference sheets with information about cultures not typically encountered in your organization, but that can be accessed quickly when needed. Many Web sites deal with cultural diversity—simply type "cultural diversity in healthcare" into your favorite search engine for an array of options. Here are two that are helpful:

- **EthnoMed** (*http://ethnomed.org*) offers information about cultural beliefs, medical issues, and lifestyles of immigrants to the United States. Emphasis is placed on people arriving from war-torn parts of the world.

- **Cultural Diversity in Healthcare presented by Geri-Ann Galanti** (*www.ggalanti.com/ cultural_profiles*) profiles a number of cultures including East Indian, European, Russian, Hispanic, Middle Eastern, Asian, African American, and Anglo American.

References

1. Galanti, G. 2003. *Cultural diversity in healthcare.* Retrieved April 30, 2004, from *www.ggalanti.com/cultural_profiles*.

2. Narayan, M. 2003. "Cultural assessment and care planning." *Home Healthcare Nurse* 21(9): 611–618.

3. Nisha, D., Giordano, J., and France, N. 2007. "Cultural diversity teaching and issues of uncertainty: The findings of a qualitative study." *BMC Medical Education* 7(8): April 2007.

Teaching Strategies
for Adults

Chapter 10
Motivation challenges: Managing resistant learners

Learning Objectives

After reading this chapter, the participant will be able to:

- Recognize education barriers that can cause resistance to learning
- Implement strategies to motivate the adult learner

One of the basic principles of adult learning is that adults are self-directed learners. But what happens when adults direct themselves *not* to learn?

All staff development specialists face the challenge of motivating learners who don't want to participate in a given learning activity. These resistant learners are restless, sometimes rebellious, and often sullen. Their muttering and body language clearly tell you that they do not want to participate, whether the setting is a classroom, on-the-job, or in a distance-learning environment. Their attitudes affect other learners, making it difficult to establish and maintain a positive learning environment. They may even encourage open rebellion among participants. How can you deal with this problem and maintain a positive attitude?

First, let's review some fundamental guidelines for teaching adults (About.com 2007):

- Identify learners by name when in a classroom setting or when addressing e-mails.
- Clarify objectives and expectations.
- Clarify consequences (if any) for failure to meet learning objectives and expectations.

- Be punctual. Begin and end learning activities on time whether in a classroom setting, during a teleconference, or during live Web-based training. If the learning activity is presented in a distance-learning format, make sure that all necessary resources are available when and where you say they will be.

- Be prepared, no matter the setting or the teaching strategy.

- Provide opportunities for learners to ask questions and receive feedback at regular intervals. This is especially important when implementing distance-learning activities. To communicate with distance learners, set up specific office hours, communicate via e-mail, or create the opportunity for live chats with the help of your information systems department.

Resistant Learners

There are three factors about resistant learners that you must recognize and accept. First, the problem of resistant learners will never vanish. As long as you are in the education business, you will face learners who seem set to hamper learning activities. This is one of the ongoing challenges that all staff development specialists face.

Second, don't blame yourself for someone's lack of motivation. True, there are poorly designed and implemented learning activities. However, in most cases, you are not responsible for a colleague's willingness to learn. Evaluate the effectiveness of your programs and make improvements as indicated by their success or lack thereof. But don't assume the responsibility for your colleagues' behaviors and beliefs—and don't let anyone else make you responsible for them, either (Hequet 2004, Snell 1998). Your responsibility is to enhance organizational effectiveness and job performance by providing effective, well-designed, and well-implemented learning activities and to strive to continually improve your education products and services.

Finally, you will not improve motivation by ignoring or accepting the resistant learners' attitudes and behaviors. This will only make the disruption of the educational activity worse, interfere with willing participants' ability to learn, and hamper your ability to effectively carry out education. You may need to make some unpopular decisions and take difficult actions to deal with these challenges. This chapter offers steps to deal with resistant learners. They are not always easy, nor are they 100% effective, but they should help diffuse the negative atmosphere created by resistant learners.

Strategies for Motivation

Use what you know about adult learning, learning styles, and differences among generations and cultures to assess the quality of the programs you develop. Armed with this knowledge, answer the following questions when developing strategies for motivating resistant learners.

What evidence can you provide to justify learning activities? Is it clearly understood why education is important or mandated?

You may assume that everyone knows why education (e.g., new procedures, customer service training) is necessary, but remember not everyone has access to the same information, no matter how effectively you believe you and other managers communicate. Part-time employees, employees who spend a lot of time on the road (e.g., visiting nurses, liaison nurses), and employees who work evenings, weekends, and holidays do not receive the plethora of information conveyed to those who work day shifts. And no matter how hard a busy organization tries to communicate with its staff members, the communication is not always effectively transmitted or accurately received.

Therefore, it is up to you and your staff development colleagues to clarify the importance of, as well as the rationale for, educational activities. You can do this verbally in classroom settings, in writing, or via audio means for distance-learning activities. Reiterate these explanations in your objectives.

Think about learning activities in terms of staff development evidence-based practice. Have you really thought about justifying education using concrete, objective data? Do you use these data to explain the importance of particular learning activities? Remember that learners are some of your most important customers. Imagine that you are selling your learning activities. To do so, you must convince participants that the activities will have a positive impact on:

1. Patient outcomes

2. Job performance

3. Organizational effectiveness

To do this, you must present your evidence in ways that convince and motivate (Avillion 2007). Objectively analyze your learning activity by gathering data and verifying conclusions:

- What data do you have that supports the need for a particular learning activity? Where did you find these data? How did you collect them? Are there additional sources of data that you are not utilizing?

- How do you analyze data? How often do you perform this analysis?

- What benchmarks or best practices did you identify from your data analysis?

- What effect do you anticipate this learning activity will have on your organization, its patients, and its employees?

- How will you communicate these findings to learning activity participants?

How can you use evidence to either justify implementation or prevent it from being developed/implemented?

It is important to recognize whether a learning activity is truly necessary. You have probably been asked to develop an education program to solve a problem that is not the result of insufficient knowledge. For example, suppose several physical rehabilitation nursing units are having difficulty administering medications on time. Adverse occurrence reports indicate that the cause of these events is a system problem, not a knowledge problem. Medications are scheduled to be administered when many of the patients are away from the units receiving physical therapy and other treatment modalities. It is not possible to change therapy schedules, but it is possible to change routine administration times. Working with the pharmacy, these units were able to change the routine times put in place by the rest of the hospital. For example, *once a day* means 9 a.m. on most units but means 8 a.m. on the rehabilitation units.

Suppose management wanted you to conduct a program about correct medication administration to solve this problem. The nurses would certainly be resistant, and you would be frustrated trying to plan a program that was not needed. Before rushing to develop a program, investigate the issues involved in the problem. By doing so, you may be able to avoid wasting your time and the time of potential learners. In this case, you would learn the discrepancy in medication administration times and the problem would easily be solved.

Have you identified your audience?

If you work for a large organization, it is not possible to personally know all of your learners. But there are steps you can take to get to know your audience and their learning styles:

- When you have the opportunity to observe learners (e.g., during a learning activity, on the job, or in the cafeteria), do your best to establish a friendly rapport. Learners are more likely to be honest and cooperative if they feel they know you.

- Pay particular attention to the general learning style and the generation of your learners.

- Use what you know about these characteristics to plan programs.

- Notify your learners as far in advance as possible about education offerings (Dickerson 2003). There will always be the need for just-in-time training, but the needs of adult learners must be considered. They deserve advance notification to arrange schedules, plan for child care if program attendance requires extra hours at work, and do any prerequisite/prelearning activity preparation.

- Emphasize how the content of education programs and services can be applied to their areas of practice and how it can improve job performance.

Are your learners afraid of repercussions if knowledge is not acquired?

Most organizations have certain knowledge requirements, such as attaining CPR certification or advanced cardiac life support (ACLS) certification for critical care personnel. If certification is not attained, employees will lose their jobs or be demoted. Fear of adverse consequences can make people feel negatively toward and behave differently during learning activities. Although you cannot alter the consequences, you can provide a supportive environment, ensure that the activity is well-designed and appropriately implemented, and work with management to provide tutoring as appropriate.

Is the educational content offered in manageable increments?

Too much information relayed at too rapid a pace does not allow learners time to absorb information. A complex education program, such as ACLS or spinal-cord injury rehabilitation should be broken into increments, and a variety of teaching techniques should be used.

Does the staff development specialist have credibility? Is the content presented accurately?

Learners resist (and may resent) unqualified educators presenting content. For example, a critical care course presented by someone who has no critical care experience, or a computer-based learning program relating to the pathophysiology of spinal cord injury that contains errors or is outdated will not be received well. Adults expect to gain accurate knowledge and skills during their learning activities. Inaccurate information or unqualified presenters will generally be interpreted by learners as offensive and a waste of time (About.com 2007, Dickerson 2003).

Do you use a variety of teaching techniques?

Classroom presentations must contain more than lecture and discussion. Make sure handouts and visual aids are colorful and appealing. Implement at least one technique for each leaning style. Pay attention to the audio and visual content of distance-learning methodologies (Dickerson 2003, Hequet 2004).

Do you have an upbeat, positive attitude about education?

If you are bored or convey a negative attitude, your learners will soon be bored and negative, too. You set the tone by your body language, enthusiasm, and ability to encourage learning. This is easier done in person than in distance learning, but you can make sure that distance-learning activities are well-designed and visually and aurally pleasing.

Do learners feel comfortable in the learning environment?

The environment must be supportive and nonthreatening, regardless of the teaching method. Include questions on the performance evaluation about the emotional comfort of the learning environment. Adults who feel belittled or embarrassed will not be enthusiastic learners.

Dealing with Overt Hostility

The preceding discussion offers good suggestions for dealing with resistance among your learners, but what do you do when someone becomes downright hostile? Here are two scenarios that offer possible ways to deal with such people.

Case study 1

The disruptive learner

You are hired as the manager of staff development for a 500-bed community hospital. One of your first actions is to ensure attendance and participation at mandatory education classes, particularly those that deal with workplace safety. The CEO's administrative assistant, Jennifer, has never attended these mandatory training sessions. However, based on recommendations from accrediting organizations, all employees are required to participate in these classes.

Jennifer is angry and resistant. Some components of the program were offered in a classroom setting, and Jennifer arrives about five minutes before the first class begins. She sits in the back of the room and immediately begins to complain loudly about having to attend this program. Some of her complaints include, "I don't see why I have to attend this ridiculous program. I work for the CEO and have better things to do," and "I never had to go to programs before, why should I start now?"

You use a variety of teaching techniques, including fun activities. However, with Jennifer in the room, the atmosphere becomes hostile. You try to be upbeat and positive, clarifying why these programs are important to both employees and customers. You encourage class input and make sure staff expertise and life experiences are acknowledged. However, Jennifer keeps muttering about being bored and complaining that the class activities are ridiculous. Most of the other participants are disgusted by her behavior, but a few of them begin making negative comments, too. What else can you do?

This type of scenario is frustrating and, sadly, not uncommon. However, you cannot allow one person to destroy the learning experience for everyone else. An organization that values education will support you during such situations. Consider arranging a small group activity for the other learners and asking Jennifer to speak with you in private. You don't want the conversation to embarrass her—or you. Tell her that it is obvious she doesn't want to participate and is upset. Ask whether there is anything you could do to help.

If her response is, "Yes, get me out of here," tell her the choice is hers to make. She could stop disrupting the class and show some consideration for her colleagues or return to her work. Always give a choice. It's up to the learner to take responsibility for his or her actions.

What if Jennifer chooses to leave? As she goes, she adds, "Just wait until I tell my boss about you!" The next day you are summoned to the CEO's office. Explain to him or her, as objectively as possible, what had happened, and state that it was Jennifer's choice to leave rather than to stop disrupting the class.

Case study 2

The violent learner

Mark, a staff nurse, arrives at your office for some tutoring in rhythm-strip interpretation. Mark has 10 years of experience as a medical-surgical nurse, but he is new to cardiac care. His new job depends on his ability to accurately interpret and identify treatment modalities for cardiac dysrhythmias. Mark needs help, but with extra work he will acquire the necessary knowledge and skills.

Mark is obviously angry when he arrives for the appointment. He refuses to sit down and says, "I've been a nurse for 10 years and never had any trouble before. It's the way this stupid course is being taught. You don't know what you're doing." He begins pacing, and you notice his fists are clenched.

In a calm, deliberate tone, you ask Mark to sit down and explain to him that you want to make this experience less frustrating for him and to help him gain the necessary cardiac-care skills. He responds by reaching across your desk, grabbing both your arms, and shouting, "I don't need your help."

What do you do? Here are suggestions for dealing with angry or violent learners (Mulvihill 2002, Snell 1998):

- **Encourage the person to sit down.** You should sit down as well. This puts you on equal eye level and helps diffuse anger.

- **Use a calm, measured tone.** Do not raise your voice or let your body language indicate anger or fear.

- **Do not take the person's anger personally.** His or her real anger may be with a spouse, another colleague, or a supervisor. The person may be feeling ill. You just happen to be the target of displaced anger. That doesn't make it any less frightening, but it does make it easier to maintain your self-control.

- **Actively listen.** Maintain eye contact. Nod your head to indicate understanding. Tell the person that you are there to help him or her, but do not allow the person to shout or threaten you. Tell the person that you will listen to any concerns and will try to help as long as he or she treats you with respect.

- **Never allow the person to stand or sit between you and the exit.** Always make sure you have a way to get out of an office or classroom. If the anger escalates and you feel you are in danger, ask the angry learner to leave your office, classroom, etc. If he or she does not comply with your request, leave the area at once.

- **Know how to get help quickly.** Don't be afraid to call out for help if you are in danger.

- **Know how to summon security personnel.** All organizations should have an emergency number to summon help. Make sure you know what to do in the event of this kind of emergency. If you anticipate that a meeting has the potential for violence, ask another colleague to be present. The presence of another person may be all that is needed to diffuse anger.

- **Report the incident.** Never allow violence—threatened or actual—to go unreported. Follow your organization's policies and procedures for reporting these incidents.

Although you cannot make someone learn or be motivated to learn, you can facilitate learning to the best of your ability. By relying on the principles of adult learning and your knowledge of the various learning styles and generational/cultural differences, you can have a significant effect on the enthusiasm of the learners within your organization.

References

1. About.com. 2007. *How to motivate adult learners.* Retrieved March 12, 2008, from *http://adulted.about.com/cs/howtoresources/ht/Motivate.htm.*

2. Avillion, A. 2007. *Evidence-Based Staff Development: Strategies to Create, Measure, and Refine Your Program.* Marblehead, MA: HCPro.

3. Dickerson, P. 2003. "Ten tips to help learning." *Journal for Nurses in Staff Development.* September/October 2003: 244–250.

4. Hequet, M. 2004. "Training no one wants." *Training* 41(1): 22–28.

5. Mulvihill, C. 2002. "Dealing with the difficult patient." Retrieved August 6, 2002, from *www.pitt.edu.*

6. Snell, N. 1998. "Stand up: Defusing the hostile trainee." Retrieved August 6, 2002, from *www.trainingmag.com.*

Chapter 11

Resourceful teaching strategies

Learning Objectives

After reading this chapter, the participant will be able to:

- Identify resourceful teaching strategies to improve education delivery
- Implement specific resourceful teaching strategies effectively

This chapter concentrates on resourceful teaching strategies appropriate for today's healthcare environment. Once referred to as "creative training techniques," the term *resourceful strategies* better fits the challenges currently facing staff development specialists.

Historically, creative teaching focused on classroom techniques (Avillion 2007). Although classroom creativity is still important, on-the-job training and distance learning have assumed equal importance in the staff development arena. You not only need to be creative, but also resourceful.

Evidence-Based Staff Development Practice as a Foundation for Resourceful Teaching

Evidence-based practice (EBP) in staff development has two stages (Oermann 2007):

1. Generating practice-specific evidence by conducting research

2. Using valid and reliable research findings (evidence) as a foundation for your own staff development practice

To successfully implement EBP, you must:

- Question the effectiveness of your current staff development practice

- Analyze your current staff development practice

- Based on analysis, gather evidence for the planning, implementation, and revision of your learning activities

You can't be innovative or resourceful until you identify best practices in staff development and compare your products and services to these practices.

Figure 11.1 on the CD-ROM is a proposed template for the analysis of your current programming and recommendations for resourceful teaching strategies. Use this template to analyze current offerings and to help determine whether proposed offerings are worthwhile based on evidence. This template also helps you to identify or revise resourceful teaching strategies.

Research as a Resourceful Teaching Strategy

Adults need to know why they are learning and what positive impact a particular learning activity will have on their lives. They want to have a sense of control over their learning and to feel that they are contributing to the learning process. Research is an excellent resourceful strategy that is not used often enough.

The concept of conducting research may be intimidating for some members of your organization. Misconceptions and anxiety about participating in research may trigger resistance to this teaching strategy (Clarke 2008).

You are not going to expect staff nurses, for example, to initiate and conduct a research project at the PhD level. But you don't need to hold a doctorate to participate in the research process. Select an appropriate topic based on analysis of educational needs. For example, suppose that quality improvement data show that the length of stay following left-hemisphere stroke is increasing (or develop a hypothetical situation to use as a basis for a research activity). A learning activity could be developed that:

1. Involves nurses in collecting data about this problem

2. Helps nurses to analyze the data

3. Identifies two possible solutions to the problem

4. Initiates separate types of nursing interventions in an attempt to solve the problem

5. Evaluates the outcomes of these interventions and recommends a best practice solution to the problem

You can use this strategy with your staff development colleagues as well. The goal is to conduct research in such a way that it has a positive impact and helps nurses and other healthcare professionals contribute to the body of knowledge for their specialty. A hypothetical situation can be presented in a classroom setting, as a computer-based learning project, or small group activity. Use your imagination and include research as a resourceful teaching strategy.

Accelerated Learning

Accelerated learning is the process of acquiring knowledge and skills at a rapid rate. Successful accelerated learning depends on a calm, supportive learning environment accompanied by the use of resourceful teaching strategies such as visual aids, graphics, music, imagery, and active learner participation. Providing tips to enhance memory is also integral to the accelerated learning process (Meier 2000, Pike 1994).

Advances in medical technology and disease recognition/treatment happen almost daily and thus require ongoing continuing education. Healthcare professionals must absorb large amounts of information quickly (Nicholl et al 1997, Pike 2003). Try these techniques to facilitate accelerated learning:

- **Use techniques appropriate for all three learning styles (auditory, visual, and kinesthetic).** Provide visual triggers such as flashcards, auditory triggers such as reciting information aloud, and kinesthetic triggers such as practicing psychomotor skills.

- **Incorporate the unusual.** Learners remember unusual triggers best. Learning activities should be accompanied by music, role play, games, etc.

- **Include frequent breaks during learning activities.** This is necessary whether the activity is in the classroom or part of distance learning. For example, during a computer-based program, alternate presentations of information with interactive sessions.

- **Use music styles to set the mood.** Different types of music promote different types of learning moods. For example, slow pieces such as baroque and chamber music promote tranquility and a relaxed mood. Jazz can stimulate and pep up the mood, as do marches and music with percussion instruments (Craig 1996). When you call for catalogues, be sure to ask about the policy for using music as part of your education programs:

  - LifeSounds: 888/687-4251

  - The Mozart Effect Resource Center: 800/721-2177

  - Superlearning: 640/731-4569

- **Create course themes.** Themes must be carefully chosen and should create a relaxed and fun atmosphere, tie course content together, trigger enthusiasm and energy, and stimulate creativity. Consider themes such as solving a mystery, a day at the beach, a scavenger hunt, or a television show.

Resourcefulness in the Classroom

The classroom setting is usually popular with adult learners. It allows for interaction, discussion, demonstration, teamwork, role play, and other activities that stimulate learning. Let's review ideas for enhancing the learning environment in the classroom.

Room setup

How are your classrooms arranged? Do you have the flexibility to physically alter the setting? If you do, consider the following:

- Avoid arranging an aisle in the center of your learners' seats. The center is really the best place to sit for viewing the educator and any audiovisual materials. Place aisles to either side of your audience whenever possible.

- Traditional classroom settings consist of rows of desks or tables facing the front of the room. The educator faces them, either standing at the front of the room or behind a podium or desk. This formal structure can be intimidating for adults. Consider options such as U-shaped groupings of tables or desks, square or rectangle arrangements, or a series of round tables. Round tables are particularly conducive to small group activities.

- Avoid standing behind a desk or podium. This keeps you at a psychological distance from the learners.

- When choosing a room, be aware of the noise distraction from other classrooms, heating and air-conditioning systems, and noise outside the building (e.g., from construction). Change location if necessary. If that is not possible, make sure speakers and audio equipment can be heard above the outside noises. Use a portable microphone to help you in these situations.

- Lights with dimmers are an asset. They allow minimal light for note-taking when using various audiovisuals without producing glare.

- If you have input into the selection of wall, floor, and chair covering, remember that floral, striped, or vivid colors such as red are distracting. Avoid them. Solid shades in soft colors are preferable.

- Before your programs, check out the sound level. Stand in various parts of the room, ask your presenters to speak, and check the audio portion of any equipment.

- Do not use chairs with rigid backs (e.g., stack chairs). The backs of chairs should support the lower back and be sturdy. When possible, choose chairs that are easy to move.

- If possible, arrange electrical outlets to be placed every 6 feet along the walls. Ideally, telephone jacks should be located next to the outlets for conference calls, audioconferences, and computer hookups. Think about cable television outlets when making design plans. The popularity of cable modems has taken hold.

Figure 11.2 on the CD-ROM is a chart that organizes tips for audiovisual, or AV, aids. These tips include those aids used in distance learning (Avillion 2007, O'Conner 2001).

Group activities

Group activities are welcomed by Baby Boomers and members of Generations X and Y if they believe they will have fun while participating. Veterans may be more hesitant. Prior to initiating group activities, make sure the learners have the necessary knowledge and skills to effectively participate. Remember, you don't want learners to be embarrassed in front of their colleagues.

Group leaders help stimulate learners during activities. You and other staff development specialists can function as group leaders, or the learners themselves can select a leader from each group. Group leaders need to be sure that all members have a chance to participate and that no one learner dominates the group. They must also:

- Make sure that the group activity will enhance learning. Don't include group activities unless they serve a purpose.

- Sit participants at round tables.

- Give clear directions, both verbally and in writing. Explain the purpose of the group activity, objectives, and what each group is expected to accomplish and present to the entire class at the end of the activity.

- Remember that music can help set the tone of the activity. For example, classical music can aid meditative activities and rousing marches can stimulate. Again, make sure to choose royalty-free music.

- Avoid giving the impression that you or the group leaders are judging or eavesdropping on the groups.

- Set the tone by being upbeat and enthusiastic.

Possible group activities
Debate

Two groups, under the tactful moderation of the staff development specialist, present two sides of an issue. An interesting tactic is to ask members to defend the opposite side of the debate issue. Twists can help learners understand both sides of an issue and helps diffuse the potential for uncomfortable disagreements.

Panel

The use of a panel strategy involves assigning learners to separate groups. Each group functions as an expert panel, discussing a particular issue in front of the other groups. The purpose is to allow group members to present specific concepts and ideas and to answer questions from the audience, which consists of groups of other panels. Each panel has an opportunity to present its viewpoints and to deal with questions or concerns from others. A moderator facilitates the presentation and ensuing discussions.

Role playing

Role playing is most effective when acting out an interpersonal skill or human relations situation. Each role play should be followed by analysis and evaluation of the situation. Remember that Baby Boomers may be reluctant to participate in role play.

Demonstrations and return demonstrations

These are especially effective when psychomotor skill acquisition is necessary.

Resourceful teaching is an essential ability of the staff development specialist. Selection of these types of strategies should be based on evidence. One of the most interesting challenges to this resourcefulness is how and when to use distance learning. The next chapter focuses on distance learning and how to decide what learning activities are most appropriate for teaching at a distance.

References

1. Avillion, A. 2007. *Evidence-Based Staff Development: Strategies to Create, Measure, and Refine Your Program.* Marblehead, MA: HCPro.

2. Clarke, D., and Sawatzky-Dickson, D. 2008. "Increasing understanding of nursing research for general duty nurses: An experiential strategy." *The Journal of Continuing Education in Nursing* 39(3): 105–111.

3. Craig, R., Ed. 1996. *The ASTD Training and Development Handbook. A Guide to Human Resource Development.* 4th ed. New York: McGraw-Hill.

4. Meier, D. 2000. *The Accelerated Learning Handbook.* New York: McGraw-Hill.

5. Nicholl, M., and Rose, C. 1997. *Accelerated Learning for the 21st Century.* New York: Dell Publishing.

6. O'Conner, M., and Virgil, G. 2001. "Teaching/learning methodologies." In A. Avillion (Ed.): *Core Curriculum for Staff Development.* 2nd ed. 231–261.

7. Oermann, M. 2007. "Approaches to gathering evidence for educational practices in nursing." *The Journal of Continuing Education in Nursing* 38(6): 250–257.

8. Pike, R. 1994. *Creative Training Techniques Handbook.* 2nd ed. Minneapolis, MN: Lakewood Publications.

9. Pike, R. 2003. *Creative Training Techniques Handbook.* 3rd ed. Minneapolis, MN: Lakewood Publications.

Chapter 12
Distance learning

Learning Objectives

After reading this chapter, the participant will be able to:

- Differentiate the various types of distance learning

- Gather evidence to select the most effective distance-learning strategy

When asked about learning preferences, many learners say they prefer the live, interpersonal, face-to-face classroom setting. They like the interaction among learners and educators, and many admit they enjoy the break in their work routine. However, all healthcare staff development specialists know that it is becoming increasingly difficult to allow learners to take time away from their work. So what's the answer? Finding the right mix of classroom and distance, self-learning strategies.

A popular term to describe this mix is *blended learning*. Blended learning is the combination of many types of learning activities (e.g., classrooms, on-the-job training, distance learning, skills labs, etc.) to best meet learners' needs (Johnson 2003, Paloff et al 1999). This chapter focuses on distance learning, because the need for education that learners can access at times that are convenient to their schedules continues to grow. Distance learning encompasses a wide range of techniques that are implemented "at a distance" from a centralized education location. The fastest growing distance-learning strategy is e-learning. The process of converting some classroom learning activities to e-learning activities is commonplace.

Deciding which Programs to Convert to e-Learning

Here are suggestions regarding the types of programs that would be effectively presented via e-learning (Johnson 2004).

- **Programs that require strict consistency of content:** for example, Health Insurance Portability and Accountability Act of 1996 training, infection control, and similar mandatory courses.

- **Programs that must reach large numbers of employees quickly:** for example, aspects of orientation and new hospital- or departmentwide policies or procedures.

- **Learning activities that affect small numbers of employees infrequently:** for example, education needed to work within a specific specialty (e.g., recovery levels of traumatic brain injury).

When determining the most appropriate way to delivery learning activities, start by logically and objectively evaluating the strengths and weaknesses of each delivery system. Not all programs are suitable for conversion to e-learning. Assess your current and potential programs and document the findings of your analysis. This does not have to be a complicated process. Figure 12.1 is a possible template you can use to document your findings and gather evidence to support your decisions. Remember, evidence-based practice in staff development relies on such evidence. This approach not only justifies your decisions but facilitates your ability to effectively communicate the rationale for your decisions to others (Avillion 2007).

Figure 12.1

Sample template for evaluating distance learning

Program	Current format (Anticipated format)	Strengths	Weaknesses	Evidence

Here is a breakdown of the template in Figure 12.1:

- *Program* column: Identify the specific program you are evaluating.

- *Current format* column: Identify exactly how you currently present this program or how you would like to present it. Be specific. Include information about necessary equipment (e.g., DVD player, PowerPoint capability), handouts, faculty, etc.

- *Strengths* and *weaknesses* columns: Identify the strengths and weaknesses of the current or anticipated approach.

- *Evidence* column: What evidence have you gathered about the program or proposed program? What is the impact of the program? What supports your decision to continue to offer the program in its current format? What supports your decision to change to an e-learning format?

Documenting what you know about your programming helps you to make an informed decision and facilitates your ability to justify such decisions to colleagues and administration.

Remember that as Baby Boomers retire, the technologically savvy Generations X and Y are taking over the workplace. These learners expect education to be fast, flexible, and convenient. They also expect technology to play a major role in education. It's what they've grown up with.

Starting a Distance-Learning Initiative

Do your learners have the knowledge and skill to access and participate in e-learning? Perhaps the first e-learning course should be an assessment of learners' computer competency. In fact, computer literacy should be part of your organization's competency program. It will soon be difficult to find a job that does not require at least minimal computer skills.

There are many e-learning companies that specialize in healthcare education. These companies frequently contract with particular healthcare systems to provide e-learning at reduced costs for their clients. Just type in "continuing education for healthcare professionals" in your favorite search engine and you will be amazed by the number of responses you receive. Be sure to use the phrase *continuing education*. If you just use *education*, you're likely to receive most of your hits from colleges and universities publicizing formal academic programs.

Strategies for Blended Learning

Research indicates that learners who are enthusiastic about distance learning are highly motivated, self-disciplined, and serious about obtaining education. To facilitate the use of e-learning among all employees, help them redefine their concepts of learning environments.

Although the picture of a formal classroom setting immediately comes to mind when you ask staff to think about education, learning environments are without geographic limitations. Your learners may be down the hall, in the next state, or in another country. The new learning environment is one in which learners share a common purpose and communicate through the written word as well as the occasional personal encounter. Holding conference calls via computer enables you to both see and write to your students. In the near future, such virtual classrooms allowing written, visual, and audio interaction will become commonplace. Generations X and Y are the most likely generations to quickly adapt to e-learning as a normal education source.

Distance learning can be used as the sole educational medium or in combination with classroom work. Consider using distance education for self-tutorials or for preliminary work in acquiring new knowledge and psychomotor skills. After learners are comfortable with didactic knowledge and pass a written assessment of this knowledge, they could move to a clinical laboratory setting to practice and demonstrate newly acquired psychomotor skills. You may be able to create challenge exams that employees new to the organization or a specialty can take and thus opt out of certain aspects of classroom orientation.

Never attempt to develop e-learning without the support and assistance of your organization's e-learning experts. These are the people who will prevent you from wasting significant time and money on developing programs that your organization's electronic systems cannot sustain.

Distance-Learning Approaches

Let's review some of the specific distance-learning approaches. Cost and equipment availability are important considerations when developing any type of distance learning (Buhmann 2001).

Television, video, and DVD

Closed-circuit television and videos/DVDs provide cost-effective education at the learner's convenience. Newer systems eliminate the need for video recorders and separate DVD players by incorporating necessary technology within the closed-circuit system.

Staff development departments can produce their own DVDs if people in the organization have the expertise to professionally produce, record, edit, and narrate a program. Poorly produced programs are ineffective. Local television stations may provide resources in exchange for acknowledgment in the program. Remember that narration is critical to the success of any program broadcast over closed-circuit television or implemented as a DVD.

Teleconferencing and video conferencing

Teleconferencing enables an unlimited number of participants at different locations to participate in a learning activity via a telephone system. Video, DVD, and computer communications may be part of the conference.

This type of education is quite convenient because it can be made available within an organization or in an individual's home. For this approach to succeed, equipment must be high quality. The educator presenting via teleconference must be skilled at facilitating communication exchange among participants and have the ability to be verbally effective. This type of education is generally synchronous in real time.

Computer conferencing

Electronic bulletin boards offer the ability to conference without satellite or long-distance charges. Asynchronous conferencing allows learners to post and read messages at their convenience. Virtual conferences allow immediate participation during live events. Live or real-time conferencing allows participants to take part in live discussions by posting messages via keyboard entry and watching a meeting transcript on the computer screen.

Professional associations are good resources for people who need the convenience of posting and reading messages at their convenience without being forced into a particular location or time frame. Many associations use electronic bulletin boards as a mentoring mechanism.

Computer-based learning

CBL is any type of training that uses a computer as the basis for education delivery (Lewis et al 2007, Travale 2007). CBL is also referred to as "computer-assisted instruction" (CAI) and "computer-based instruction" (CBI). It is essential that learners have a mechanism for obtaining help easily (Flagg et al 2008). Learners who encounter problems with CBL (e.g., Web site being down, can't locate the "help" feature) will not likely pursue this type of education.

CBL has many subtypes, such as interactive video discs, CD-ROMs, and DVDs. Many companies specialize in online learning. Such companies often offer continuing education for healthcare professionals and are eager to partner with healthcare organizations.

References

1. Avillion, A. 2007. *Evidence-Based Staff Development: Strategies to Create, Measure, and Refine Your Program.* Marblehead, MA: HCPro.

2. Buhmann, J. 2001. "Technology and staff development" in A. Avillion (Ed.): *Core Curriculum for Staff Development.* 2nd ed. Pensacola, FL: National Nursing Staff Development Organization. 304–341.

3. Flagg, J., Saarmann, L., Seidman, R., and Sweeney, N. 2008. "The keys to successful online continuing education programs for nurses." *The Journal of Continuing Education in Nursing* 39(1): 34–41.

4. Johnson, G. 2003. "Brewing the perfect blend." *Training* 40(12): 30–34.

5. Johnson, G. 2004. "Conversion anxiety." *Training* 41(2): 34–40.

6. Lewis, P., and Price, S. 2007. "Distance education and the integration of E-learning in a graduate program." *The Journal of Continuing Education in Nursing.* 38(3): 139–143.

7. Palloff, R., and Pratt, K. 1999. *Building Learning Communities in Cyberspace.* San Francisco: Jossey-Bass.

8. Travale, I. 2007. "Computer-assisted instruction for novice nurses in critical care." *The Journal of Continuing Education in Nursing* 38(3): 132–138.

Chapter 13

From novice to expert

Learning Objectives

After reading this chapter, the participant will be able to:

- Determine teaching strategies using Benner's levels of competency as a framework
- Correlate Benner's levels of clinical competency with staff development expertise

In 1984, Patricia Benner, PhD, RN, published the results of a descriptive nursing study that identified five levels of competency in clinical nursing practice (Benner 1984). Although based on dialogues with nurses, this framework can be applied to almost anyone who works in healthcare. As you plan your programs, think about learner needs based on their experiences in their chosen professions.

Using Benner's Framework for Program Planning

Brief descriptions of each level of learner identified by Benner are offered as a trigger for your planning. Following the descriptions are suggested teaching tips for that level.

Level I: Novice

The novice is a beginner in his or her chosen profession. Novices have no experience as professionals in their work-related environments. They need objective, concrete learning situations. Although they possess the intellectual knowledge of academic training, they need opportunities to apply their knowledge as skills in the actual work setting. They also need a supportive environment with mentors who are eager to help colleagues enter the healthcare setting.

Teaching considerations

- Offer case studies to allow novice learners to practice translating knowledge into practice.

- Encourage mentorships with more experienced nurses.

- Offer programs that add to learners' basic knowledge. Develop didactic programs combined with opportunities to discuss translating knowledge into practice to meet their needs.

- Give novice learners opportunities to demonstrate newly acquired psychomotor skills.

Level II: Advanced beginner

Advanced beginners are able to demonstrate marginally acceptable performance. They have dealt with enough real-life situations to recognize their most meaningful aspects and intervene appropriately in similar situations. They begin to rely on guidelines formed from their own experience.

Teaching considerations

- Offer advanced-beginner learners activities that give them a chance to use their experiences to acquire new knowledge.

- Offer interactive e-learning, lecture/discussion, case studies, and role play opportunities to improve organizational skills and prioritize workloads.

- Advanced beginners benefit from mentoring opportunities.

Level III: Competent

Competent clinicians have worked in the same or similar environments for at least two to three years. They view their actions in terms of long-range plans as they organize and prioritize tasks that must be completed.

Teaching considerations

- Give competent-level learners opportunities to develop leadership skills.

- These learners value programs that provide updates and recent advances in their specialties.

- They enjoy interactive learning and more complex case studies than the previous two levels.

- Allow them opportunities to partner with proficient and expert learners (see following descriptions) during learning activities.

Level IV: Proficient

Proficient clinicians look at situations as a whole rather than breaking them down into guidelines or isolated tasks. They are able to anticipate events in given situations based on their past experiences. They can plan ahead with a fair amount of certainty.

Teaching considerations

- These learners benefit from learning activities that present a challenge.

- Provide opportunities to develop instincts and intuition such as interactive case studies presented via e-learning.

- The previous three levels look to proficient-level staff for assistance. Proficient-level employees need to develop leadership skills, so leadership training is a good idea.

- Provide formal mentorship training.

Level V: Expert

Experts no longer rely on analytic principles, nor do they need to refer to past experiences to grasp the important elements of a situation. Experts have an instinctive, intuitive grasp of each work-related situation. They are able to quickly focus on the crux of a problem and intervene appropriately without considering a large range of alternative solutions.

Teaching considerations

- Experts need to have quick access to advances in their given specialties.

- They need to implement leadership skills and help others acquire such skills.

- Programs on how to facilitate learning among their colleagues are appropriate.

- Experts must be able to help assess the quality of their colleagues' work.

- Classes on quality management and performance improvement are appropriate.

Benner's levels of expertise are also applicable to the practice of staff development.

See Figure 13.1 on the CD-ROM which correlates each level with specific characteristics and identifies interventions to take when facilitating the professional growth of staff development specialists in your department (Avillion 2007).

References

1. Avillion, A. 2007. *Evidence-Based Staff Development: Strategies to Create, Measure, and Refine Your Program.* Marblehead, MA: HCPro.

2. Benner, P. 1984. *From Novice to Expert.* Menlo Park, CA: Addison-Wesley Publishing.

Unit 4

Addressing Specific Staff Development Challenges

Chapter 14
Compiling needs-assessment data

Assessing learners' needs can become an exercise in futility. Have you ever been faced with a mountain of data that is disorganized and makes little or no sense? Needs assessments, although critical, need to be built into existing systems so you don't waste time and effort setting up additional methods of data collection.

Many staff development departments still conduct some type of annual or semiannual needs-assessment survey. A sample form from such a survey can be found in Figure 14.1. Before conducting a similar survey, be sure that the time and effort it takes to collect and analyze these types of data is worth the effort.

There is space in the template to add disciplines, job titles, or more questions, if you wish. Answers to the questions about factors that help and hinder job performance can be used to trigger education topics, especially if they reflect data obtained from other sources. If you are distributing the survey for learners to complete at their leisure, add a deadline for completion and instructions about where they should bring the completed survey.

Figure 14.1

Sample needs-assessment form

Please complete the following education needs-assessment survey. The staff development department will use this information to plan programs for the coming year. These programs will be designed to improve job performance and patient outcomes. Thank you for your participation!

Date: _____

Name (Optional): _____

Discipline: RN_____   LPN_____   CAN_____   PT_____   OT_____

SLP_____   SW_____   Pharmacist_____

Information systems specialist_____

Organizational development specialist_____

Manager (please indicate discipline)_____

Years of experience in your discipline: _____

1. Identify three education programs that you would attend to help you improve your job performance.

_____
_____
_____

2. Identify three things that interfere with your ability to do your job.

_____
_____
_____

3. Identify three things that help you to do your job.

_____
_____
_____

Figure 14.1

Sample needs-assessment form (cont.)

4. Are you comfortable attending education programs that are offered via computer based learning?

     Yes ___ No ___

If not, what would help you to become more comfortable?

_____

_____

_____

5. How do you most prefer to obtain education?

Classroom setting_____   Computer-based learning_____

Video/DVD_____   Audiotapes or audioconferences_____

Skills lab_____   Self-learning packets_____

E-mail updates_____   On-the-job demonstration_____

Other

_____

_____

_____

6. Please let us know if you have additional comments or suggestions to improve staff development services.

_____

_____

_____

Needs assessments are conducted to identify and prioritize learning needs, assess the level of interest in particular education topics, differentiate learning needs from systems or performance problems, and meet accreditation standards. Data come from many sources. You need to be able to track information in a logical, concise manner.

Here are suggestions to ensure an ongoing flow of relevant information concerning learners' educational needs:

1. **Establish a computerized system of documenting and monitoring education needs.** Work with your information systems department or investigate some of the education tracker software from your vendors.

2. **Determine how you will categorize education topics.** For example, suppose you decide to alphabetize your list of topics, recording not only the topic, but also how many times it was requested and the source of the request (e.g., program evaluations, needs-assessment forms, quality-improvement meetings). Where would you file a request such as "Psychological impact of multiple sclerosis (MS) on the patient and family"? Would you record it under mental heath issues, family needs, or MS? Pick the broadest, easiest to recognize category—in this case, MS. If you have more than one person entering needs-assessment data, be sure that everyone involved understands how to categorize and record identified learning needs.

3. **Establish a system for data collection.** Identify the sources of your information. These should include learners, administration, management, performance evaluations, quality-improvement data, and identified trends in healthcare.

4. **Review data on a regularly scheduled basis.** Although most organizations plan their programming at least six months in advance, you need to allow time for the addition of learning activities triggered by urgent patient care or other organizational needs.

Using Data from Program Evaluations

Your goal should be to make data collection as easy as possible. Most education program evaluations include questions about additional learner needs such as, "What education topics would you like to see presented in the future?" This is too vague. You will get all kinds of responses, including requests that have nothing to do with education (e.g., "We need more employee parking."). When requesting information about learners' education needs on program evaluations, consider rephrasing the question(s) to gain the data you really need. For example, ask staff to identify:

- Specific education topics that would improve their ability to do their job

- Education programs that they would enjoy attending

- Specific education topics that would improve their ability to provide patient care

These questions will help you differentiate between programs designed to improve job performance and those that may simply be topics of interest without job relevance.

Data from Quality Improvement Findings

How do you access quality improvement data that are relevant to education planning?

Ideally, you or a staff development colleague should be a member of the quality improvement committee. As a member, you will have firsthand knowledge of trends that affect patient outcomes and other organizational services. You will also have the opportunity to teach other members of the committee how to differentiate between learning needs and systems and performance problems. For example, an increase in patient falls on a particular unit does not necessarily indicate a lack of employee knowledge.

Work with the quality improvement committee to analyze the problem. Has there been a change in patient acuity or staffing patterns? When do the majority of falls take place? Are staff members assessing patients' needs inaccurately? By answering these questions, you can determine whether the problem is due to a systems failure, a lack of knowledge or implementation of knowledge, or a combination of both. Once this is determined, you can take appropriate intervention.

Record learning-needs data obtained from this committee under the umbrella of quality improvement. Then compare these data with needs identified by learners and identify similarities and differences. This will also help you to determine whether staff members are aware of quality improvement issues within the organization.

Data from Performance Evaluations

Performance evaluations are confidential. You should not have access to evaluations throughout the organization. So how do you obtain necessary data?

An organization that values education will help you establish a system for collecting this data. Performance evaluations are conducted frequently in any organization. A logical way to obtain these data is to establish a regular system of collection. Build it into each department's quality improvement program. Managers should be required to summarize learner needs obtained from performance evaluations and give this information to you quarterly. Managers can also alert you to any trends needing immediate attention whenever they are identified. Compare these findings with quality improvement data and data obtained from learners themselves.

Other Sources of Data

At this point, you have established an ongoing system of data collection from three critical sources: learners, quality improvement findings, and performance evaluations. But suppose you want more information, such as the learners' years of experience in a given profession or what factors hinder or help them perform their jobs.

Obtaining this information could be part of an annual needs-assessment survey. Only collect data that will be helpful to you. For instance, do you really need to know on which unit someone works? You already have information about trends and needs from performance evaluations and quality improvement findings that indicate problem locations. If you have a genuine need for this information, fine. But don't ask for it simply because it's always been part of the needs-assessment form.

It's usually a waste of time and effort to distribute needs-assessment forms via intraorganizational mail or even electronically. Most people just don't consider completing an annual needs-assessment form a high priority. Instead, look for events that large numbers of employees attend. For example, does your hospital offer Nurse Week events or hold an employee appreciation day? Consider distributing needs-assessment surveys at major events and offer a simple reward (e.g., pens, discount coupons) for those who complete the survey. Make it easy for yourself. Find an event that already gathers large numbers of employees and incorporate your needs assessment into the process.

Figure 14.2 is a template for organizing needs-assessment data. This is especially helpful if you decide to forego the annual needs-assessment survey format. This type of documentation allows you to keep track of your education needs and still have an easy source of evidence pertaining to needs assessments.

Figure 14.2

Organization of needs-assessment data

Data type	Data source	Mechanism for collection	Frequency of data collection	Summary of findings

Following are explanations for the type of information appropriate for each column in Figure 14.2:

- **Data type:** Record the what type of data you are collecting—for example, number of patient falls, number of requests for a program on how to deal with abusive patients, etc.

- **Data source:** Document the specific source of data, such as adverse occurrence reports, annual needs-assessment survey, or performance evaluations.

- **Mechanism for collection:** Exactly how do you obtain these data? Do managers send you a list of identified education needs based on the performance of their staff members? Is a staff development specialist a member of the risk management committee? If so, does he or she obtain a list of the adverse occurrence reports according to type and number?

- **Frequency of data collection:** Note how often you collect each type of data.

- **Summary of findings:** Summarize the overall findings from data collection to use as evidence and justification for program development.

Chapter 15

Orientation

Learning Objectives

After reading this chapter, the participant will be able to:

- Discuss orientation strategies that facilitate the orientee's organizational assimilation

Most staff development specialists groan when asked to evaluate and update their orientation programs. One of the few certainties in healthcare staff development is that orientation is in a constant state of revision.

If you have enough staff development specialists in your department, assign one or two the responsibility for ongoing assessment of orientation. This helps to keep track of the success (or lack of success) of orientation efforts. Answer the following questions as you begin your assessment process:

- Are you responsible for orienting a specific department or do you have responsibility for some aspects of orientation for all new employees?

- What particular aspects of orientation are your responsibility?

- Who provides departmental orientation? Do you have any responsibilities for clinical orientation? If so, do you have clinical educators who perform this duty?

- How often do you hold orientation classes? Is orientation regularly scheduled, or is it done on an as-needed basis?

- How do new employees evaluate the orientation process?

The answers to these questions determine how you design your orientation program. Try to arrange a regular time or times each month for orientation. Because of current staffing shortages, you may be pressured to orient new employees on demand. This can be disastrous. Clinical preceptors/mentors need time to orient colleagues properly, and so do you. Inadequate orientation inevitably leads to early resignation and a significant loss of the organization's time and money.

Arrange orientation classes and self-learning activities in conjunction with other programs as often as possible. For example, if there is a certain skill that all employees must demonstrate annually (e.g., proper use of fire extinguishers), arrange for these monitored demonstrations to take place when new employees are present. This allows both new and current employees to meet a mandatory requirement without the staff development department having to schedule numerous, unplanned demonstrations.

One of the most logical ways to improve your orientation program is to develop a systematic, ongoing process of evaluation. The focus of this evaluation is gathering evidence to identify best practices in orientation for your organization (Avillion 2006, Avillion 2007).

Cost

Determine the cost of your orientation program. Work with your human resources department to analyze costs in relation to turnover for at least a sixth-month period. Depending on the size of your organization and the number of employees hired monthly, you may need to analyze costs more frequently. If your turnover is low, annual analysis may be sufficient (Avillion 2006). Use the following methods to determine costs:

- Calculate the time spent delivering orientation. Include classroom instruction, time spent grading tests, answering questions (including questions received via e-mail), assisting with distance learning, and time spent delivering education that coincides with orientation (e.g., annual mandatory training classes, competency assessments, etc.). Multiply the hourly salary of those involved by the number of hours spent teaching, facilitating learning, and answering questions.

- Calculate the number of hours spent interacting with managers, preceptors, and orientees about schedules, concerns, and other issues related to orientation. Multiply the number of hours by the hourly salary of those staff development specialists involved.

- Calculate the time spent preparing orientation education materials (McCarthy et al 2001). Some good rules of thumb are:

  - Program planning: 5 hours

  - Program development: 15 hours

  - Review, revision, and pilot testing: 5 hours

  - Clerical support: 5 hours

- Determine the cost of office supplies, including handouts, self-learning modules, etc.

- Determine travel costs. If you work in a multisite facility, you many need to travel to various geographic locations within your health system. Include reimbursement costs such as mileage and gas as part of the cost of your orientation.

- Include the cost of support from other departments (e.g., guest speakers).

Learning Styles and Teaching Methods

You also need to assess the effectiveness of teaching methods in conjunction with various learning styles and generational differences. Answer these questions as part of your ongoing orientation assessment:

- How are the needs of orientees with different learning styles addressed? Do you include strategies that enhance visual, auditory, and kinesthetic learners' orientation experience?

- What types of teaching methods do you employ? How effective are your blended learning strategies? Do you incorporate distance-learning strategies?

- How do you address the needs of learners with specific generational characteristics?

- How do you address the needs of a maturing RN work force? Remember: The average age of the RN in the United States is 46.8 years old. Have you considered the needs of this population when planning and implementing orientation?

Data Analysis and Best Practice Identification

Figures 15.1 and 15.2 deal with orientation analysis and can be used as templates to help you answer the preceding questions, calculate costs, and organize your methods of data collection and best practice identification. They serve as guides since each organization has its own needs and culture. Feel free to use and adapt these templates to help you to analyze and revise your orientation program.

Figure 15.1

Template for orientation analysis

Cost

Delivery _____

Interaction _____

Preparation _____

Staff development clerical assistance _____

Office supplies _____

Travel _____

Subtotal: _____

Support from other departments _____

Preceptor time _____

Advertising _____

Interview costs _____

Grand total: _____

Cost efficiency

Actual % of budget devoted to orientation _____

Optimal % of budget that should be devoted to orientation _____

Difference: _____

Figure 15.1

Template for orientation analysis (cont.)

Teaching methods:

Classroom:

_____

_____

Distance learning:

_____

_____

Other:

_____

_____

Future options:

_____

_____

Generational learning strategies

Identify strategies for each of the following generations.

Veterans:

_____

_____

Baby Boomers:

_____

_____

Generation X:

_____

_____

Generation Y:

_____

_____

Future options:

_____

_____

_____

Figure 15.2

Orientation data collection

Data collection	Findings	Recommendations for program revision	Best practice identification
Data source (e.g., orientee evaluation, results of competency assessment)			

Now, let's look at a few issues that have a significant impact on orientation and some suggestions for their incorporation in orientation.

Preceptorship

If clinical orientation is the responsibility of clinical educators or staff nurse preceptors, make sure these individuals have received formal training in preceptorships, leadership, and adult education. It is highly recommended that those who function as mentors/preceptors receive financial compensation for these extra responsibilities. The most successful preceptor/mentor programs are part of a clinical ladder that makes attainment of these roles part of a job promotion (Gloe 2001). Do the following when developing your preceptor training program:

- Establish a specified amount of clinical experience as a requirement for becoming a preceptor/mentor.

- Select individuals who have demonstrated not only clinical competence, but also a genuine desire to help their colleagues excel at their jobs.

- Do not force anyone to become a preceptor/mentor. Candidates for this role must want such responsibilities.

- When designing a curriculum for preceptors/mentors include the following topics:

  - Principles of adult education

  - Learning styles

  - Generational differences

  - How to offer constructive criticism

  - How to evaluate clinical performance

  - Leadership principles

  - Communication skills

Some of the preceptor's responsibilities include:

- Establishing a short-term relationship for the purpose of helping the orientee to successfully complete orientation

- Assisting during orientation in learning unit policies and procedures

- Planning appropriate clinical experiences for the orientee

- Providing feedback to the orientee related to competency, skills, role, and interpersonal interactions

Mentors

Mentors are not preceptors. Preceptors assume a short-term fixed role for the purpose of helping a new employee to orient successfully to a specific department. Mentors, however, establish a relationship of indeterminate length for the purpose of acting as a role model on a long-term basis (Gavlac 2007). A mentor functions as a coach who helps the mentoree grow professionally (McCarthy et al 2001).

Some of the mentor's responsibilities include:

- Teaching about the politics and subtle cultural nuances of an organization

- Acting as a sounding board for decision-making and problem-solving

- Introducing the mentoree to significant people within and outside of the organization

- Offering encouragement and supportive feedback

- Offering information to help the mentoree avoid career hazards

Mentor programs have correlated positively with job satisfaction. Consider establishing a mentor program to help all levels of employees—not just orientees—enhance their professional development. Note that mentorships are not specific to the orientation period. In fact, new employees may not be ready for mentoring until they have some basic understanding of their roles and responsibilities.

Competency-Based Orientation

Design your orientation as a competency-based system. Such a system acknowledges and builds on previous knowledge and skills. The orientee should be able to demonstrate knowledge and test out of certain areas of competency. For example, experienced pediatric nurses should not have to sit in a classroom or participate in extensive e-learning on pediatric medication administration. They should have the opportunity to take a challenge test and, upon successful completion of the test, move forward in the orientation.

There are limitations to developing and implementing this type of orientation program. The initial development takes time and is costly. There must be an adequate way to document competency (use the same competency documentation forms that have already been established for assessment of current employees). However, after the initial program is in place, advantages far outweigh the limitations (Gloe 2001):

- New employees are presented with clear, measurable performance expectations
- Competency demonstration is based on department-specific knowledge and skills
- Orientation time is decreased for experienced professionals
- Competency-based orientation establishes an objective system to document competence
- Preceptors/mentors and managers have a comprehensive foundation for performance evaluation
- The cost of orientation is decreased because new employees are able to test out of areas in which they are competent
- New employees have a consistent orientation program

In summary, do not react in a knee-jerk fashion every time someone requests changes in your orientation program. If you conduct an ongoing analysis of orientation by collecting and evaluating data, monitoring costs, and using a variety of teaching strategies, you should be able to gather evidence to justify your current program and make necessary revisions and innovations when applicable.

References

1. Avillion, A. 2006. *Designing Nursing Orientation: Evidence-Based Strategies for Effective Programs.* Marblehead, MA: HCPro.

2. Avillion, A. 2007. *Evidence-Based Staff Development: Strategies to Create, Measure, and Refine Your Program.* Marblehead, MA: HCPro.

3. Gavlac, S. 2007. "Centralized orientation: Retaining graduate nurses." *Journal for Nurses in Staff Development* 23(1): 26–30.

4. Gloe, D. 2001. "Implementation of learning activities." In A. Avillion (Ed.) *Core Curriculum for Staff Development.* 2nd ed. Pensacola, FL: The National Nursing Staff Development Organization (NNSDO). 261–302.

5. McCarthy, M., and Storm, C. 2001. "Role of the performance coach in staff development." In A. Avillion (Ed.) *Core Curriculum for Staff Development.* 2nd ed. 561–578.

Chapter 16
Mandatory education

Learning Objectives

After reading this chapter, the participant will be able to:

- Discuss the concept of mandatory training

All organizations mandate particular education components for employees. These types of required learning activities are usually conducted on a regular schedule (e.g., annually). Mandatory programs include but are not limited to those dealing with safety issues, infection control, violence in the workplace, and the Health Insurance Portability and Accountability Act of 1996 (HIPAA) issues. As mentioned in previous chapters, streamline your efforts whenever possible to meet the needs of more than one group of learners at the same time.

If you have selected an interactive computer-based learning package for some of your mandatory training, make sure your learners know how to use these programs and that they have adequate access to computers.

How do you deal with attendance at required classes? Many organizations have arranged mandatory monthly learning activities. If you do this, make sure your orientation program coincides with the day(s) that mandatory training is being offered. Arranging a particular day(s) each month allows employees and orientees alike to fulfill mandatory requirements.

Your mandatory classes are probably a blend of classroom, demonstration, and self-learning methods (including e-learning). Set up a classroom and arrange for didactic components and skills demonstrations to be offered at regular intervals throughout the day. (If you work for a large health system you may need to offer these classes around the clock). Make a number of computers and other self-learning tools (e.g., video or DVD players) available, too. Most employees find it difficult to leave their work areas for an hour at a time on different days to fulfill mandatory training requirements. However, if you arrange daylong events, employees can schedule for an education day, fulfill their mandatory education requirements at once, and will not need to worry about returning to their work areas.

Incorporate competencies into your mandatory training events. This enables objective measurement and documentation of skill or knowledge accomplishment in addition to program attendance. Whenever possible, use a computerized system to track education attendance.

Consider providing opportunities for employees to test out of particular mandatory education classes. For example, experienced clinicians do not necessarily need to sit in a class watching a video and hearing a didactic lecture about CPR. Consider giving these employees the opportunity to take a written test and demonstrate CPR without sitting through a lengthy program. (Check with your sponsoring CPR organization, usually the American Heart Association or the Red Cross, to make sure that this option meets its recertification requirements.)

Flexibility is important when helping administrative staff to attend mandatory training. Distance learning and flexibility are critical. Most staff development specialists have faced the challenge of making mandatory education as convenient as possible for people such as the chief executive officer, vice president of nursing, or the medical director.

Do what you can to make mandatory training less tedious and more enjoyable for all staff. Incorporate role play, case studies, and other group activities when possible. Vary the techniques you use from year to year. You may need to stay within the same format (e.g., a daylong event, test-out options, computer-based learning) but change the way specific content is delivered. If you used a lecture discussion technique for one component of mandatory training this year, switch to a case-study approach next year. Although the content may be similar, the approach can change. This will keep both you and your learners from becoming bored.

Remember that your organization may add or delete certain components of mandatory training based on organizational needs and accrediting standards. Be flexible. Avoid becoming too rigid about fixed time frames for specific components of mandatory education. Remember to ask learners to evaluate mandatory education classes; they may have good suggestions to improve the delivery of this type of education.

Chapter 17
Inservice education

Inservice education generally refers to simple, short-term programming that meets an immediate need. The best example of inservice education is on-the-job training, sometimes referred to as just-in-time training (Ellis 2003, Puetz et al 2001). In other words, it's learning what you need when you need it. Inservice education often involves the need to master a new piece of patient care equipment quickly, provide quality patient care for a patient with an unusual/unfamiliar illness or injury, or implement a new/updated policy or procedure immediately.

Inservice education is a quick response to changes in your work environment. These types of education needs produce a special challenge for staff development specialists. They are usually unexpected, allowing little time for program preparation and implementation, and require swift demonstration and validation of competency. Successful implementation of inservice education requires the following:

- A ready and willing educator who is adequately qualified to present information
- Learners who are ready and willing to learn and eager to help their colleagues learn
- The availability of necessary equipment, documents, etc.

Fulfilling these requirements is not easy. Let's review common examples of inservice training and how to implement them successfully.

New Policies or Regulations

The immediacy of inservice education is reserved for those policies and regulations that affect patient outcomes; patient, visitor, or employee safety; and accreditation status. If such policy and regulation changes are not complex, their success may require only that employees read and sign documents to verify that they understand and accept the changes.

If this is the case, don't waste your time planning programs that consist of an educator reading a document to a group of learners. Within large organizations, e-learning may be the answer for the majority of employees—posting the new policy or regulation on the organization's Web site or distributing e-mails may solve the problem. If your organization does not have the capability of having employees use an electronic signature to indicate they have read and understood the new guidelines, copies of the guidelines can be e-mailed to department managers. Managers can then post the guidelines and an accompanying signature sheet in work areas, and employees can sign that sheet after they have read the new policies or regulations. Managers of small departments may choose to present the new information during a staff meeting and ask their employees to sign off then.

Try to ensure consistency in how employees indicate their understanding and acceptance. To that end, you can develop a template like the one in Figure 17.1 that can quickly be customized and distributed to the appropriate work areas for the purpose of documenting your inservice education.

Figure 17.1

Template for policy/regulation inservice documentation

Date: _____

Department/unit: _____

Distribution of the following new organizational policy(ies)/regulations: _____

_____

_____

The attached document(s) indicate a change in or a new way of providing products and services to our patients, families, visitors, and/or employees.

After you have read these documents, indicate that you understand and accept these changes or additions by dating and signing below. If you have any questions, please contact your departmental manager.

It is required that each employee reads the attached documents and signs his or her name by

_____

Date	Signature	Title

New Equipment

A scenario that commonly triggers a need for new equipment inservice education is the transfer or admission of a patient to your organization who is accompanied by a new, unfamiliar piece of equipment necessary for his or her care.

How can you implement training and ensure staff competency? Determine whether anyone within your organization is familiar with this equipment. If the patient is in fact a transfer, inquire whether someone from the transferring hospital can accompany the patient to help educate staff. Another option is to contact the vendor leasing or selling this equipment. Most vendors have preprinted guidelines for equipment use and are often willing to provide inservices to staff around the clock. Whether or not you actually do the teaching in this scenario, you must document training and competency. Keep a blank template in your computer to do so. Figure 17.2 is a suggested template for the documentation of inservice pertaining to new equipment or procedures.

Figure 17.2

Inservice documentation form for new equipment

Date: _____

Time: _____

Competency: _____

Type of equipment: _____

Instructor(s): _____

After observing accurate demonstration of _____, the following learners demonstrated competence in the use of _____

_____
Instructor's signature, time, and date

Date   Time   Learner's signature and title

_____

_____

_____

_____

_____

_____

_____

_____

_____

_____

_____

_____

_____

_____

_____

_____

Unusual Illness or Injury

The clinical patient care team will most likely develop protocols and treatment modalities. However, you will probably need to help your colleagues by researching unfamiliar diseases or injuries. Following are Web sites that will help you when researching this type of challenge:

Centers for Disease Control and Prevention (www.cdc.gov)

"The Centers for Disease Control and Prevention (CDC) is recognized as the lead federal agency for protecting the health and safety of people—at home and abroad—providing credible information to enhance health decisions, and promoting health through strong partnerships. CDC serves as the national focus for developing and applying disease prevention and control, environmental health, and health promotion and education activities designed to improve the health of the people of the United States."
Source: CDC Web site.

National Institutes of Health (www.nih.gov)

"The National Institutes of Health is the steward of medical and behavioral research for the Nation. It is an Agency under the U.S. Department of Health and Human Services."
Source: NIH Web site.

American Association for Clinical Chemistry (www.labtestsonline.org)

This site offers information on a wide variety of lab tests, including rarely ordered tests and information about how to interpret findings.

The Food and Drug Administration (www.fda.gov)

This site offers a wealth of information about drug trials, approvals, warnings, and cautions.

PubMed (www.pubmed.gov)

"PubMed, a service of the National Library of Medicine, includes over 14 million citations for biomedical articles back to the 1950s. These citations are from MEDLINE and additional life-science journals. PubMed includes links to many sites providing full text articles and other related resources."

Source: PubMed Web site.

References

1. Ellis, K. 2003. "Top training strategies." *Training* July/August 2003: 31–35.

2. Puetz, L., and Zuel, S. 2001. "Educational planning." In A. Avillion (Ed.) *Core Curriculum for Staff Development.* 2nd ed. Pensacola, FL: The National Nursing Staff Development Organization (NNSDO): 199–229.

Chapter 18

Continuing education

Learning Objectives

After reading this chapter, the participant will be able to:

- Discuss ways to deliver continuing education

Continuing education is generally defined as learning activities designed to enhance an employee's professional growth and development (Puetz et al 2001). These programs, like all learning activities, are ultimately expected to contribute to improvement of job performance and customer satisfaction.

Classroom Setting

Specific continuing education programs are often identified by learners as educational needs. However, if they are not directly connected to training mandates, competency, or other requirements, it is doubtful that large numbers of learners will be able to leave their work to attend. Every staff development specialist has spent long hours developing excellent programs only to find few, if any, learners in the classroom. Enthusiastic administrative and management backing is usually the most effective way to improve attendance. Although blended learning is now a norm when developing learning activities, there are still some occasions when only a classroom setting will do (Fennimore 2002). Here are some tips to enhance attendance:

- **Create enthusiastic advance publicity.** Select a topic that is bound to trigger interest, such as bioterrorism preparedness or, for oncology nurses, information about the most recently Food and Drug Administration–approved chemotherapeutic agents:

  - Publicize the dates and times of the program

  - Offer the program more than once and during different shifts

  - Make use of your organization's computer technology to announce programs

  - Make sure these announcements are visually interesting and add audio effects

  - Use action verbs to describe what the program is about and how your learners and the organization will benefit from knowledge and skills acquired during this program

  - Use bulletin boards located in strategic places such as inside the cafeteria and hospital entrances to promote the program

  - Use bold, colorful words and illustrations to announce your programs

- **Give the learners an added incentive.** You can purchase pens and notepads engraved with virtually anything these days. If your program is about customer service, have notepads printed with the phrase "The Best in Customer Service!" Giveaway incentives are cheap and easy to order. Just type "personalized business gifts" into your favorite online search engine for a multitude of contacts.

- **Encourage word-of-mouth publicity.** Ask learners with whom you have a good rapport to help you promote your programs.

- **Offer credits.** When possible, offer continuing education credits for your programs. This includes programs offered as distance-learning activities.

Blended Learning

Consider offering your continuing education programs in several formats. Here are some ideas for delivering continuing education via distance-learning methodologies:

- **Independent, printed study modules.** These could be similar to those offered in professional healthcare journals. If your organization has an organizational newsletter, consider publishing self-study continuing education modules in it.

- **Computer-assisted programs.** These programs can be entertaining and promote interactive learning.

- **Teleconferences.** Popular with healthcare professionals who have limited time and resources to obtain continuing education, this is typically a useful method.

- **Partnerships with Web-based healthcare education companies.** As mentioned previously, type "continuing education for healthcare professionals" into your favorite online search engine for an amazing number of results. These companies might be able to take some of the design and coordination burden off your shoulders.

- **Live chats.** These Web-based programs allow participants to interact with learners throughout the world. Organizations that have recently sponsored live chats include the Oncology Nursing Society and CancerresourceRN. Contact professional associations to find out whether they are offering live chats with experts.

Finally, make sure you follow the basic steps of good program planning. Remember to:

- Assess needs
- Identify clear, measurable objectives
- Develop a content outline based on these objectives
- Develop content using the outline as a road map
- Market the program enthusiastically
- Implement the program using the most appropriate teaching modalities
- Evaluate the effectiveness of the learning activity

Evaluation is the step in the educational process that best demonstrates your effect on organizational effectiveness. The next chapter discusses, in detail, evaluation methodologies that help you to demonstrate your worth to your administration, management, and colleagues.

References

1. Fennimore, L. 2002. "Delivering distance learning." In B. Puetz and J. Aucoin (Eds.): *Conversations in Nursing Professional Development*. Pensacola, FL: Pohl Publishing. 317–328.

2. Puetz, L., and Zuel, S. 2001. "Educational planning." In A. E. Avillion (Ed.): *Core Curriculum for Staff Development*. 2nd ed. Pensacola, FL: The National Nursing Staff Development Organization (NNSDO). 199–229.

Assessing the Effectiveness
of Education

Chapter 19

An overview of the evaluation process

Once upon a time in staff development, many education programs were offered in classroom settings, attendance was good, learners enjoyed the activities, and your organization thought you were doing a great job.

So this idealistic viewpoint is not *completely* accurate— but there was a time when staff development performance was judged by the amount of programs offered, attendance numbers, and the satisfaction of those who attended.

Today, you are still expected to offer many programs, promote good attendance, and provide learning activities that participants enjoy. However, this does not necessarily mean that you are doing a great job. In the current healthcare environment, you must also demonstrate to the organization that it is worth the time, money, and effort to support education and promote the recruitment and retention of qualified staff development specialists.

Staff development specialists are responsible for the effectiveness of their education products and services. You must provide evidence that education improves job performance and enhances patient outcomes. To do this, you need an objective system of data collection and analysis. You need to produce evidence that links staff development products and services to improved job performance, better patient care, and a positive impact on the organizational bottom line. You must also use this evidence to close the gap between ideal staff development practice and the reality of practice within your organization (Abdulhadi et al 2001).

The fact that an educator is consistently rated as "highly qualified" and "a good presenter" is important, but it does little to demonstrate the effect education has on organizational effectiveness. However, if you can document a 40% decrease in patient falls as a result of using knowledge gained from learning activities, for example, you not only helped improve patient safety, but also justified the existence of your education programs.

Arguably, the reduction of patient fall rates does not prove that a specific learning activity was directly responsible for diminished occurrence. However, you can provide objective evidence that indicates a probable link between education and improved outcomes. How do you collect this evidence? You need to determine what types of evaluation strategies to use. Many staff development specialists refer to these strategies as levels of evaluation, each indicating a progression in complexity. Collecting the data you need requires more than one level of evaluation (Abdulhadi et al 2001). The succeeding chapters describe each evaluation strategy and when and how to implement them (Avillion 2007):

- **Level one: Reaction/learner satisfaction.** How do the learners feel about the activity? What do the results indicate about the learners' satisfaction with the program?

- **Level two: Learning/knowledge acquisition.** What did the participants actually learn as a result of the learning activity?

- **Level three: Behavior.** Did the learners' job performance change based on the learning activity?

- **Level four: Results/impact.** How did behavior changes affect organizational effectiveness?

- **Level five: Return on investment (ROI).** How did the learning activity financially affect the organization? What investment in the actual cost of a learning activity was made and what was the return benefit(s) generated by it?

It is not necessary, nor is it efficient, to conduct all five types of evaluation on every program you offer. But you should have a solid understanding of how each can affect the future delivery of your learning activities.

Using Evidence in Educational Evaluation

Gathering and analyzing data from these five levels of evaluation is, and has been for some time, necessary. However, it is what we do with the data that has changed compared to prior evaluation efforts. Think in terms of evidence, not merely data. Identify not only the effect that education has on organizational performance, but determine best practices and benchmarks for your practice. Use these findings as a means of adding to the body of knowledge that is staff development.

Evaluation of education is a "concept and process, is the process of weighing, interpreting, and subsequently making judgments about the data collected from multiple components of educational programming" (Menix 2007). Evaluation is, more explicitly, an ongoing process for the identification of evidence that:

1. Links education to specific organizational outcomes

2. Facilitates identification of best practices and benchmarks

3. Forms the basis for research in staff development

4. Adds to the body of staff development knowledge

As you shift the focus of your department to one that is grounded in evidence-based practice, evaluate each of your current program offerings. Figure 19.1, found in *Evidence-Based Staff Development: Strategies to Create, Measure, and Refine Your Program*, is a program analysis template that helps you to logically look at the status of your programs in terms of evidence.

This type of program analysis helps you to understand how you collect data, find evidence, and determine conclusions for your programs. The following chapters deal specifically with each level of evaluation and how you can build on program analysis to evaluate your programming.

Figure 19.1

Program analysis template

Task	Findings	Comments/Recommended revisions
Identify: • Existing data sources • Method of collecting data • Method of documenting data • Frequency of data collection • Additional sources of data that need to be, but are not currently, in use		
Describe: • The mechanism for analyzing data and how often this occurs • Frequency of program revisions based on identified evidence		
Determine: • Best practices identified via data analysis • Benchmarks compiled from best practices		
Verify conclusions by: • Reviewing history of best practice conclusions • Reviewing the literature to verify conclusions		
Identify current or potential research projects that correlate with best practices and benchmarks		

Reference

1. Abdulhadi, L., and Hull, E. 2001. "Program evaluation and return on investment." In A. Avillion (Ed.) *Core Curriculum for Staff Development.* Pensacola, FL: The National Nursing Staff Development Organization (NNSDO). 343–360.

2. Avillion, A. 2007. *Evidence-Based Staff Development: Strategies to Create, Measure, and Refine Your Program.* Marblehead, MA: HCPro.

3. Menix, K. 2007. "Evaluation of learning and program effectiveness." *The Journal of Continuing Education in Nursing* 38(5): 201–210.

Chapter 20

Level one: Reaction/learner satisfaction

Learning Objectives

After reading this chapter, the participant will be able to:

- Describe level one evaluation

At the reaction/learner satisfaction level, the extent of learner satisfaction with the education activity is examined. This information is sometimes referred to as a happiness index (Abdulhadi et al 2001, Kirkpatrick 1998). Reaction is insufficient as the sole method of evaluation, but it is still extremely important. If learners are bored during the learning activity, feel the material was either too basic or too complex, or believe that the instructor was unqualified or boring, their written and word-of-mouth complaints will quickly destroy the value of a particular education event. The reaction evaluation also provides important information about the physical learning environment, such as whether lighting is adequate, acoustics are good, etc.

Evidence-based practice (EBP) mandates that you analyze data to gather objective evidence for your decisions pertaining to learner satisfaction (Avillion 2007). A useful evaluation process requires that you make judgments about your program (JCEN 2003). In the case of reactive data, be prepared not only to address issues such as equipment, comfort, and satisfaction, but also to use evidence to review the faculty who prepare and deliver the learning activity.

The Reaction Form

A typical reaction form, whether for classroom or distance education, needs to capture the date and time of the event, program title, instructor, and objectives. Fill in the title, instructor's name, and objectives in advance. This ensures consistency and enables the learner to complete the form quickly. By including the objectives, you make it easier for learners to focus on evaluating them—a critical aspect of reaction data. Even though you may verbally explain the objectives and include them on slides or handouts, it is well worth the effort to write the objectives directly on the form beforehand.

Do not ask for information unless you plan to use it to analyze the success of the learning activity. For example, before you ask learners to identify their profession and work location, decide how you are going to use that information. Are you comparing satisfaction among various disciplines? Do you need to know how many learners participate from specific departments and units? If you don't need the information, don't ask for it. You will have plenty to do analyzing the data you really need (Avillion 1998).

Ask how well participants were able to achieve each specific objective. Ask which objectives (if any) were not achieved from the learners' viewpoints. Find out whether the instructor was both interesting and knowledgeable. He or she may be extremely entertaining but ill-prepared or have inadequate knowledge about the education topic—you need to know if that's the case.

Make sure the educator allowed adequate time and opportunities for discussion and questions. You also need to know whether materials such as handouts, audiovisuals (AV), etc., were useful. Additionally, ask learners to evaluate how well they could read handouts and see and hear any AV aids used during the program. The quality of these items greatly affects learners' satisfaction and ability to achieve objectives. If they cannot hear the instructor, or if the video was of poor quality, you need to know. Also give learners an opportunity to rate the comfort of the seating arrangements and classroom temperature.

Because there are questions specific to both classroom and distance programs, two templates are presented in this chapter. One is for classroom reaction and another is for reaction to distance-learning activities.

Included on the CD-ROM is Figure 20.1, a template for a simple reaction form for the classroom setting. Feel free to customize the version of this tool.

Distance-learning activities require much of the same feedback you solicit from classroom activities. Add questions concerning the type of distance-learning technique used and how effective that technique was as a learning activity.

The distance-learning evaluation form, Figure 20.2 included on the CD-ROM, offers suggestions for the evaluation of reaction to a distance-learning experience.

Remember that although it is important, reaction data does not provide evidence that learning took place. Conducting just a reactive evaluation is not adequate. You must, at the very least, move to the next level and assess the learners' knowledge gain.

References

1. Abdulhadi, L., and Hull, E. 2001. "Program evaluation and return on investment." In A. Avillion (Ed.) *Core Curriculum for Staff Development*. Pensacola, FL: The National Nursing Staff Development Organization (NNSDO). 343–360.

2. Avillion, A. 1998. *The Redesign of Nursing Staff Development*. Pensacola, FL: The National Nursing Staff Development Organization (NNSDO).

3. Avillion, A. 2007. *Evidence-Based Staff Development: Strategies to Create, Measure, and Refine Your Program*. Marblehead, MA: HCPro.

4. JCEN. 2003. "Administrative angles: Evaluation." *The Journal of Continuing Education in Nursing* 34(6): 247.

5. Kirkpatrick, D. 1998. "Great ideas revisited." In D. Kirkpatrick (Compiler) *Another Look at Evaluating Training Programs*. Alexandria, VA: ASTD. 3–8.

Chapter 21

Level two: Learning/knowledge acquisition

Just because learners loved participating in a particular program doesn't mean they actually learned anything. And, after all, knowledge acquisition is the fundamental purpose of any learning situation. Therefore, how can you efficiently and effectively measure learning?

Your objectives provide the basis for how you evaluate learning. For instance, if the objective is to achieve competence in a psychomotor skill, then safe, accurate demonstration of skill acquisition can measure learning. If the objective is to achieve intellectual, didactic knowledge, then a written test may be the best way to measure learning (Abdulhadi et al 2001, Avillion 1998).

However, to demonstrate that learning actually took place, develop an objective before-and-after approach. For example, if you use a written test as the measurement tool, ask learners to complete the test before and after the learning activity.

When preparing written pre- and posttests, consider the following:

- **Multiple choice tests are the easiest to grade.** Essay questions may be appropriate for some critical-thinking stimulation, as are case studies and clinical scenarios. However, time is usually limited, and theses types of tests are time-consuming to grade. Multiple choice tests have the further advantage of being objective, while essays, case studies, etc., require significant subjective analysis.

- **Avoid multiple component answers (also commonly referred to as *multiple multiple questions.*)** These are test items that give choices such as "all of the above," "none of the above," or "a and c." There should be one correct answer for each question.

- **True and false questions are not the best indicators of knowledge.** Keep these types of questions to a minimum, if at all.

The pretest must be done tactfully. Emphasize that the learners' score (or skill demonstration) will be used to demonstrate that learning took place. Assure them that it will not be shared with anyone other than the learner and the educator. No penalties should be involved with the pretest. In fact, if a skill is completely new, record that none of the learners had any experience with this particular skill. This avoids clumsy, embarrassing attempts to perform a psychomotor activity with which the learners are totally unfamiliar.

After you determine the best way to assess knowledge/skills before and after the learning activity, consider the following as part of your evaluation process:

- How clear are your instructions for the completion of pre- and postlearning tests? This is especially important for distance-learning activities when the only way to explain this issue is via the written word or as part of an audiotape.

- Are written materials prepared at the appropriate reading level for the learners?

- Do your written testing materials indicate that employees whose native language is not English are unable to understand what is required of them? (If this is the case, use this information to justify funding to offer classes in English as a second language.)

- Are employees whose native language is not English able to follow verbal instructions during psychomotor skill acquisition and demonstrations?

- Do employees understand why it is important to demonstrate learning?

Suppose a large department such as nursing has recently undergone extensive education to institute a complex new treatment regimen that also requires a new psychomotor skill. You have a small staff development department and are depending on many formal and informal nurse leaders (who have already acquired this skill) to observe accurate demonstration of this new skill. Consider the following points:

- Are these nurse leaders' evaluations consistent? Do they know the exact objectives and how achievement is to be demonstrated?

- Have you made written guidelines available for these nurse leaders? Written guidelines help to ensure consistency of evaluation.

- Have these nurse leaders received any training in dealing with adult learners?

- What happens if someone fails to achieve competence in this new skill? Is extra training available?

Develop a written checklist to accompany guidelines so competency is evaluated on a step-by-step basis. The person doing the evaluation must sign and date the checklist, as does the employee being observed. This documentation must be kept with the employee's education records. When observing a psychomotor skill, use a checklist similar to the one in Figure 21.1.

Figure 21.1

Demonstration of competency achievement form

Date: _____

Objectives:

_____
_____
_____

Competency demonstration:

Step 1 _____

Step 2 _____

Step 3 _____

Step 4 _____

Observer comments:

_____
_____
_____

Competency was achieved: _____
Observer's signature

_____
Learner's signature

Competency was not achieved: _____
Observer's signature

The following steps will be taken by the learner to achieve competency:

_____
_____
_____

_____
Learner's signature

Observer comments:

_____
_____
_____

Learner comments:

_____
_____
_____

Evidence of learning plus the reaction form demonstrates program value to a certain extent. However, an even better way to demonstrate program value is to obtain evidence that the learner actually applied the new knowledge/skill in the work setting (Avillion 2007). Evidence that knowledge has been acquired is necessary—but not sufficient—when seeking justification for decisions or rationalizing program development.

References

1. Abdulhadi, L., and Hull, E. 2001. "Program evaluation and return on investment." In A. Avillion (Ed.) *Core Curriculum for Staff Development*. Pensacola, FL: The National Nursing Staff Development Organization (NNSDO). 343–360.

2. Avillion, A. 1998. *The Redesign of Nursing Staff Development*. Pensacola, FL: NNSDO.

3. Avillion, A. 2007. *Evidence-Based Staff Development: Strategies to Create, Measure, and Refine Your Program*. Marblehead, MA: HCPro.

Chapter 22

Level three: Behavior

Learning Objectives

After reading this chapter, the participant will be able to:

- Gather evidence to evaluate behavior

This level involves assessing learners' behavior and the actual use of new knowledge/skills during job performance. Behavior should demonstrate the transfer of new knowledge and skills to the actual work setting. This level of evaluation takes more time and effort than the previous two levels (Avillion 1998, Kirkpatrick 1998).

Using new knowledge/skills requires the support and encouragement of management and administration. Ask yourself, "Do employees, including managers and administrators, understand how new knowledge and skills affect the organization?" To make it easier for learners to take on new behaviors, answer the following questions before education is offered (Avillion 2007, Kirkpatrick 1998):

- How is job performance to be affected by the new knowledge/skills?

- Has the impact of education been clearly communicated to learners, managers, and administrators?

- Does the work environment facilitate the acquisition and use of new knowledge/skills by providing necessary equipment, staffing, etc.?

How will you evaluate behavior? There are several options, including direct observation, review of documentation, and assessing the appropriateness of patient care interventions. Whichever method you choose, be sure that there is consistency throughout this level. Suppose a new patient treatment modality has recently been implemented at your organization. You have provided appropriate education, including rationale for treatment, demonstration and return demonstration of the treatment, and the essential documentation for this technique. Reaction evaluations are positive, and you have determined that learning has taken place. How then do you assess transfer of knowledge to the work setting (i.e., behavior)? Here are some suggestions:

- Review patient's medical records for accuracy in documenting new procedures and the patient's response

- Check use of any equipment that is part of the treatment modality for accuracy

- Directly observe nurses as they perform the procedure

Figure 22.1 is a template for the evaluation of behavior. However, as with steps taken to measure knowledge acquisition, there must be consistency of evaluation among those who observe, review, etc. Develop guidelines for evaluators and take the time to be sure that anyone who acts as an observer understands how to follow such guidelines. Again, a template is a useful time saver. Keep it in your computer and adapt it quickly for your level three evaluations.

Figure 22.1

Evaluation of behavior (applied knowledge)

Date: _____

Time: _____

Name and title of person being evaluated:

_____

_____

Name and title of person performing evaluation:

_____

_____

Objectives:

_____

_____

_____

Evaluation procedure results:

Medical record review:

_____

_____

_____

Equipment use:

_____

_____

_____

Direct observation of psychomotor skill:

_____

_____

_____

Evaluator's comments:

_____

_____

_____

_____
Evaluator's signature

Remedial action plan if necessary:

_____

_____

_____

_____
Learner's signature

Choose your observers carefully. Although appropriate for some observations, a nurse manager who spends the majority of her time on administrative tasks is not the best person to evaluate a new clinical skill. Observers may be peers, supervisors, or, in some cases, subordinates. The critical factors for success are that observers be objective, well-trained, and consistent in the evaluation process. Only if these conditions are met can the evidence be valid and reliable (Avillion 2007).

Behavioral evidence must be gathered in ways that are as objective as possible, such as:

- Review of specific portions of the medical record

- Analysis of nursing documentation

- Direct observation of a psychomotor skill in the actual work setting

- Direct observation of interpersonal communication in the actual work setting

- Direct observation of the performance of a new procedure in the actual work setting

The evidence is not useful if observers are using different standards to conduct the evaluation. Consistency is absolutely essential. Remember: The evidence is only as good as your evaluation process.

References

1. Avillion, A. 1998. *The Redesign of Nursing Staff Development.* Pensacola, FL: The National Nursing Staff Development Organization (NNSDO).

2. Avillion, A. 2007. *Evidence-Based Staff Development: Strategies to Create, Measure, and Refine Your Program.* Marblehead, MA: HCPro.

3. Kirkpatrick, D. 1998. "Great ideas revisited." In D. Kirkpatrick (Compiler): *Another Look at Evaluating Training Programs.* Alexandria, VA: American Society for Training and Development (ASTD). 3–8.

Chapter 23

Level four: Results/impact

Learner satisfaction has been positive, knowledge acquisition has been demonstrated, and on-the-job behaviors have changed and indicate application of new knowledge and skills. Good job! Now your CEO wants to know how these results affect the organization (Kirkpatrick 1998).

Level four evaluation takes considerable time and effort and is generally done when education programs are intended to help the organization achieve an important goal (Kirkpatrick 1998). Use the data you collected during level three as the foundation for this level of evaluation (Avillion 1998).

Let's continue with the example from the preceding chapters: Behavioral evaluation indicates that a new treatment modality has been safely and accurately learned by nursing employees who received appropriate training and education. How do you assess whether these behavior changes benefit the organization? Here are recommendations for the developing a procedure to evaluate the results.

Begin by confirming that knowledge acquisition and knowledge application (behavior) were accurately and consistently evaluated. Asking the following questions:

- Have the outcomes of patients receiving the new treatment modality improved?

- Have their lengths of stay decreased?

- Is there a decrease in nosocomial infections?

- Did health insurance reimbursement increase as a result of nursing documentation that helps to justify the new treatment?

- Did the successful implementation of this treatment enhance the organization's ability to meet accreditation standards?

- Do performance evaluations indicate an improvement in job performance?

Use the answers to these questions to establish evidence that education contributed positively to the organization. Do not work in isolation from other departments. Department/unit managers, members of the research department or research committee, and quality improvement staff are valuable resources. The data collected as part of this level is important to all of these work areas. By sharing resources and time, you and your colleagues can develop a level four evaluation method that measures impact from a variety of sources.

Presenting Your Data to Leadership

When presenting level four data, be prepared to be challenged to provide concrete proof that education was directly responsible for positive results. This type of proof is generally impossible to gather. Don't let this deter you from conducting level four evaluations. You cannot be absolutely certain whether behavior changes and corresponding results are because of education or due to another source. However, you can provide evidence that a link exists between education and results by collecting the data previously described. This is another good reason to involve your colleagues in data collection. Your evidence may indicate that education was effective and that the actions of managers or others contributed to positive results. Gather allies by explaining how your evaluation process will make them look good, too.

Do not use the word *proof* when presenting your data. It is too easily disputed. To prove an exact cause-and-effect relationship between education and results, you would have to eliminate all other factors that might have influenced behaviors. In a healthcare setting, this is nearly impossible. Use the word *evidence* instead.

Here are more examples of factors that can link education with positive organizational results:

- Decreased staff turnover

- Decreased patient falls

- Decreased medication errors

- Decreased employee injuries

- Decreased employee sick days

- Increase in customer (i.e., patient/family) satisfaction

- Increased profitability

Yet it is not enough to simply gather this type of evidence: How will you logically, confidently present your findings to peers and executive levels staff? It is not easy to present evidence that you understand so well to an audience unfamiliar with staff development initiatives. Figure 23.1 offers a template for evidence presentation. It is highly recommended that you use this template to document your findings and then use as a guide when presenting your evidence. Your department's reputation and value will surely increase when you present your findings in such a manner (Avillion 2007, Bell et al 2007).

Figure 23.1

Administrative report on staff development EBP

Program title	Needs-assessment data	Implementation method(s) and rationale	Evaluation data
Pathophysiology of Spinal Cord Injury: How to Intervene for Maximum Patient Outcomes	80% of RNs working on SCI unit requested update on this topic on annual needs assessment survey. Nurse managers of the neuro rehabilitation units noted that they documented a need for increased knowledge and application of knowledge concerning pathophysiology of SCI on 55% of RN performance evaluations. Length of stay for SCI patients on these units was 4–7 days longer than estimated in 60% of patients. Special comments: the SCI rehabilitation program is relatively new. It has existed for 18 months. 50% of the RNs are new to this specialty.	The program consists of blended learning: a computer-based learning (CBL) component and skills-demonstration component. Rationale: The decision for blended learning was based on a pilot study of two groups of RNs: Group I's continuing education was presented entirely in the classroom setting. Group II participated in CBL for the didactic portion of the course and then attended a skills lab. Successful completion of posttests and skills demonstration were as follows: Group I: 90% Group II: 95% Minor adjustments were made to the program, including better opportunities for question and answer sessions.	This program was offered over a period of six months. 90% of RNS working on the neuro rehabilitation units attended this program. 100% of participants successfully completed the posttest and skills demonstration lab. Direct observation of nurses who attended the program found that 90% applied new knowledge and skills in the work setting. Length of stay for SCI patients were as estimated upon admission to the SCI program for 98% of patients admitted following implementation of this education program. 2% of patients had longer than estimated lengths of stay compared to 60% prior to program implementation.

This sample shows how to organize your thoughts using evidence-based facts and figures to make an effective presentation. Note that data are presented using statistics relevant to the evidence. Keep your report short and factual. You want to make an impact with this evidence. Draw in the reader or listener with attention-grabbing information. Do not include unnecessary information. You should be able to present your data as compelling evidence that your department is effective and valuable.

References

1. Avillion, A. 1998. *The Redesign of Nursing Staff Development.* Pensacola, FL: The National Nursing Staff Development Organization (NNSDO).

2. Avillion, A. 2007. *Evidence-Based Staff Development: Strategies to Create, Measure, and Refine Your Program.* Marblehead, MA: HCPro.

3. Bell, D., Forsyth, D., and Pestka, E. 2007. "Outcome evaluation: Does continuing education make a difference?" *The Journal of Continuing Education in Nursing* 38(4): 185–190.

4. Kirkpatrick, D. 1998. *Another Look at Evaluating Training Programs.* Alexandria, VA: American Society for Training and Development (ASTD).

Chapter 24

Level five: Return on investment

Learning Objectives

After reading this chapter, the participant will be able to:

- Describe return on investment (ROI)

- Identify ways to conduct ROI

The purpose of this level is to demonstrate your education's effect on the financial bottom line of your department or organization. A return on investment (ROI) calculation requires a cost-benefit analysis (Abdulhadi et al 2001, Avillion 1998, Kirkpatrick 1998). This is a time-consuming process, so perform this analysis only when it is imperative for your department's (or your organization's) survival or when you must demonstrate your financial worth to the organization.

Suppose you have made extensive changes in your new employee orientation program. Your goal might be to demonstrate that these changes result in decreased turnover, decreased length of orientation, and decreased dollars spent to orient staff.

To begin an ROI study of these education changes, determine the cost of orientation under the old system. Answer the following questions:

- How long did orientation take?

- How much overtime was required to pay employees working extra shifts until new employees were able to safely assume their duties?

- How much staff development and preceptor time was spent orienting new employees? (Using their hourly wages, determine how much money was paid to staff who did the orienting and to new staff being oriented.)

- How much preparation time did it take to plan orientation programs? (Again, determine costs in salary for this preparation time.)

- How much money did supplies, equipment, etc., used for orientation cost?

- What was the turnover rate for new employees? (Determine how long you want to consider employees as new. Does it mean through probation? Within one year of employment?)

Next, answer these same questions based on the new orientation program. Ideally, you should obtain a year's worth of data—but the hectic pace of the healthcare industry will probably not allow for that much time. Use the length of time that employees are considered new as the appropriate period for data collection (Avillion 1998). In other words, if you are analyzing the new orientation program for six months, collect six months' of data under the old system.

Calculate ROI as a percentage. Divide the dollar value of the program (net program benefits) by the total cost of the training. Net program benefits are the program benefits minus the program costs. The formula looks something like this (Abdulhadi et al 2001, Avillion 1998, Kirkpatrick 1998):

$$ROI (\%) = \frac{\text{Net program benefits}}{\text{Program costs}} \times 100$$

Figure the ROI for both the new and the old orientation programs.

You can also report ROI as a simple dollar amount. Cite how much more it costs to orient new employees under the old system versus the new system in dollars by comparing expenses for such programs. You should be able to give administration a specific amount. Wouldn't it be wonderful to be able to say the new orientation system saves the hospital $25,000 quarterly? (Abdulhadi et al 2001, Avillion 1998, Kirkpatrick 1998)

Work with your financial experts to develop sound methods of evaluating ROI—not all clinicians or educators have this expertise. Financial experts are accustomed to looking at outcomes in terms of dollars and cents. Don't be afraid to seek help from your colleagues.

ROI provides evidence that education has a positive impact on the organization's financial bottom line. This level is quite time consuming and should be calculated for programs that have a significant financial impact on the organization and your department. Your goal is to acquire evidence that the benefits outweigh the costs associated with knowledge acquisition, knowledge application, and impact on patient outcomes (Avillion 2007, Bell et al 2007). Objective evidence is the goal.

References

1. Abdulhadi, L., and Hull, E. 2001. "Program evaluation and return on investment." In Avillion, A. (Ed.) *Core Curriculum for Staff Development*. Pensacola, FL: The National Nursing Staff Development Organization (NNSDO). 343–360.

2. Avillion, A. 1998. *The Redesign of Nursing Staff Development*. Pensacola, FL: NNSDO.

3. Avillion, A. 2007. *Evidence-Based Staff Development: Strategies to Create, Measure, and Refine Your Program*. Marblehead, MA: HCPro.

4. Bell, D., Forsyth, D., and Pestka, E. 2007. "Outcome evaluation: does continuing education make a difference?" *The Journal of Continuing Education in Nursing* 38(4): 185–190.

5. Kirkpatrick, D. 1998. *Another Look at Evaluating Training Programs*. Alexandria, VA: American Society for Training and Development (ASTD).

Nursing education instructional guide

Target audience:

- Staff educators
- Directors of education
- Staff development specialists
- Organizational development specialists
- Directors of nursing
- VPs of nursing
- Chief nursing officers

Statement of need:

This second edition is a guide that clinical staff directors and staff development directors can use to teach managers in an acute-care setting how to create and lead inservice education programs. The accompanying CD-ROM includes customizable tools.

Educational objectives:

Upon completion of this activity, participants should be able to:

- Describe the historical evolution of staff development
- Differentiate between traditional and contemporary staff development practice
- Implement strategic planning using mission, vision, and values statements
- Determine realistic departmental goals
- Determine realistic objectives that correlate with departmental goals
- Discuss the impact of current healthcare trends on staff development
- Describe the facets of an organizational culture of learning
- Determine the appropriate qualifications for staff development specialists in an organization
- Identify staff development specialist competencies
- Describe the various roles of the staff development specialist
- Implement the principles of adult learning in all education activities
- Describe characteristics of various learning styles
- Identify teaching strategies associated with various learning styles
- Describe the characteristics of the four generations active in the current workforce
- Identify teaching strategies that facilitate learning for each generation
- Identify ways to design effective diversity education

- Recognize education barriers that can cause resistance to learning
- Implement strategies to motivate the adult learner
- Identify resourceful teaching strategies to improve education delivery
- Implement specific resourceful teaching strategies effectively
- Differentiate among the various types of distance learning
- Gather evidence to select the most effective distance-learning strategy
- Determine teaching strategies using Benner's levels of competency as a framework
- Correlate Benner's levels of clinical competency with staff development expertise
- Describe practical strategies to obtain needs-assessment data
- Discuss orientation strategies that facilitate the orientee's organizational assimilation
- Discuss the concept of mandatory training
- List examples of inservice education
- Devise strategies for implementation of inservice education
- Discuss ways to deliver continuing education
- Identify the purposes of evaluation
- Describe the various levels of the evaluation process
- Describe level one evaluation
- Identify ways to measure level two evaluation
- Gather evidence to evaluate behavior
- Describe level four evaluation
- Describe return on investment (ROI)
- Identify ways to conduct ROI

Faculty:

Adrianne E. Avillion, DEd, RN—Adrianne E. Avillion is the author of this publication.

Accreditation/designation statement:

This educational activity for three contact hours is provided by HCPro, Inc. HCPro, Inc. is accredited as a provider of continuing nursing education by the American Nurses Credentialing Center's Commission on Accreditation.

Disclosure statements:

Adrianne E. Avillion has declared that she has no commercial/financial vested interest in this activity.

Instructions:

In order to be eligible to receive your nursing contact hour(s) for this activity, you are required to do the following:

1. Read the book

2. Complete the exam

3. Complete the evaluation

4. Provide your contact information in the space provided on the exam and evaluation

5. Submit the exam and evaluation to HCPro, Inc.

Please provide all of the information requested above and mail or fax your completed exam, program evaluation, and contact information to:

> HCPro, Inc.
> Attention: Continuing Education Manager
> 75 Sylvan Street, Suite A-101
> Danvers, MA 01923
> Telephone: 877/727-1728
> Fax: 781/639-2982

Nursing education exam

Name: _____

Title: _____

Facility name: _____

Address: _____

Address: _____

City: _____ State: _____ ZIP: _____

Phone number: _____ Fax number: _____

E-mail: _____

Nursing license number: _____

(ANCC requires a unique identifier for each learner)

1. The advent of World War II triggered:
   a. A surplus of registered nurses in the hospital setting
   b. A shift from hospital-based to private nursing practice
   c. An increase in the number of nonprofessional staff
   d. A changing emphasis on individual practitioners

2. Current practice in staff development:
   a. Places the responsibility for learning on the staff development specialist
   b. Emphasizes evidence of educational impact rather than on the quantity of products and services offered
   c. Indicates a shift from blended learning to classroom learning
   d. Reiterates the belief that promotion to leadership positions depends on clinical expertise

3. The process of determining an organization's direction is:
   a. Strategic planning
   b. Determining a vision
   c. Establishing a mission
   d. Setting goals

4. A _____describes essential functions as well as the overall reason for a department's existence.
   a. Vision
   b. Values statement
   c. Mission
   d. Objective

5. After reviewing the results of the 2004 National Sample Survey of registered nurses, staff
   development specialists should:
   a. Concentrate on the need of nurses ages 30 or under when planning programs
   b. Train faculty to speak in high-pitched tones
   c. Use at least an 8 point font in written materials
   d. Avoid having participants stand or sit for long periods of time

6. When helping to deal with recruitment and retention issues, staff development specialists realize
   that some of the most effective interventions involve:
   a. Planning "Nurse Week" activities
   b. Offering interview training
   c. Developing separate competency programs for new employees and employees who have
      been with the organization for several years
   d. Eliminate mentor programs

7. Successful development of an organizational culture of learning depends on:
   a. Informing employees that staff development specialists are responsible for making sure
      that employees acquire and apply new knowledge
   b. Prohibiting employees at the staff level from having input into the decision-making
      process
   c. Keeping change to a minimum
   d. Respecting those who are responsible for the coordination and delivery of education
      products and services.

8. Potential staff development specialists:
   a. Must have a master's degree prior to being hired
   b. Do not necessarily need leadership qualities
   c. Should be hired from outside the organization
   d. Must support a culture of learning

9. When orienting new staff development specialists, you should do all of the following EXCEPT:
   a. Incorporate staff development competencies as part of orientation
   b. Stress clinical expertise throughout the orientation process
   c. Include a component on staff development research
   d. Incorporate recognition of generational differences as part of the competency program

10. The CEO of a large metropolitan health system is recruiting for the position of Vice-President of Education. She will probably include _____ as a job requirement.
    a. A bachelor's degree
    b. Clinical expertise
    c. Business skills
    d. Licensure as an RN

11. When thinking about factors that motivate adults to learn, you should realize that:
    a. Adults respond only to extrinsic motivators
    b. Motivators such as a salary increase are not appropriate for persons involved in public service careers
    c. Increased self-esteem is an appropriate intrinsic motivator
    d. It is inappropriate to correlate education with better working conditions

12. Allison is participating in a computer-based learning course. She prefers to listen to music via headphones as she completes the course. Allison is most likely a _____ learner.
    a. Visual/spatial
    b. Kinesthetic
    c. Visual
    d. Aural

13. Linguistic learners use phrases such as:
    a. Let's touch base about this problem
    b. Let's see what we can do about this problem
    c. Let me explain this word for word
    d. Let me help you to grasp the meaning of this

14. A formal learning environment with the staff development specialist assuming the role of an authority figure is preferred by _____.
    a. Veterans
    b. Baby Boomers
    c. Generation X
    d. Generation Y

15. When planning learning activities for Baby Boomers, you should:
    a. Include role playing whenever possible
    b. Structure the activity in a formal, authoritative manner
    c. Limit the opportunity to share life experiences
    d. Include time for icebreakers

16. When planning cultural diversity education:
    a. Include every culture represented by patients or staff
    b. Prioritize based on the cultural groups that are most predominant
    c. Avoid discussing American cultural characteristics
    d. Avoid using distance-learning strategies

17. Nurses whose native language is not English:
    a. Should receive training in English as a second language
    b. Are not primary candidates for nursing positions
    c. Should be assigned only to patients who are from the same country as they are
    d. Can not be expected to communicate with persons who speak only English

18. When encountering resistant learners, the staff development specialist should:
    a. Realize that she/he is probably responsible for the learners' resistance
    b. Ignore the resistant learners' behaviors and attitudes
    c. Take steps to prevent the resistant learners' behaviors from disrupting the learning experience
    d. Refuse to allow resistant learners to participate in learning activities

19. You have been asked by your organization's administrative staff to provide continuing education and training for nurses who want to work on a proposed pediatric oncology unit. The unit is scheduled to open in two years. You should:
    a. Refuse to provide this training
    b. Explain to the nurses that even though they will not use new knowledge and skills, it is important to obey administrative directives
    c. Tell administrative that implementing the training now will lead to learner resistance
    d. Present objective evidence to administrative staff about the consequences of mandating staff to acquire new knowledge and skills that they are not able to implement

20. All of the following are strategies to help motivate learners EXCEPT:
    a. Be punctual and well-prepared
    b. Provide opportunities for learners to ask questions and receive feedback
    c. Explain the anticipated impact of the learning activity using objective evidence
    d. Explain that administration is responsible for mandating education

21. When identifying resourceful teaching strategies, the staff development specialist:
    a. Encourages the use of research as a teaching tool
    b. Avoids using music in the classroom setting because of copyright laws
    c. Avoids using the classroom setting because it is no longer practical
    d. Normally stands behind a podium or desk when teaching adult learners

22. When determining the suitability of providing distance learning:
    a. Analyze your current programming to gather evidence to support your decision
    b. Avoid documenting evaluation findings since this may cause you to commit to a particular strategy before you are ready to do so
    c. Always keep a classroom style version of the program to implement for Veterans and Baby Boomers
    d. Discourage input from Generations X and Y since they are biased in favor of distance learning

23. An appropriate intervention for an expert staff development specialist is which of the following?
    a. Opportunities to help the expert assume managerial responsible responsibilities
    b. Encourage her/him to spearhead research activities and identify best practices
    c. Provide guidelines for dealing with resistant learners
    d. Instruct her/him in the process of EBP in staff development

24. You are planning a learning activity for an audience that consists primarily of competent nurses. Competent clinicians would benefit most from:
    a. An opportunity to demonstrate psychomotor skills
    b. Working with a preceptor
    c. A chance to develop leadership skills
    d. Classroom learning

25. Which of these statements about collecting needs assessment data is FALSE?
    a. It is imperative that you distribute an annual needs assessment survey
    b. Needs assessment data are collected from a wide variety of sources
    c. Adverse occurrence reports are a useful source of needs assessment data
    d. Data concerning education needs should be as specific as possible

26. When calculating the cost of orientation, you should:
    a. Calculate the cost of the time spent planning and preparing learning activities
    b. Estimate that program development takes about 30 hours
    c. Not include travel costs associated with orientation because they have no bearing on the actual learning activities presented
    d. Not include the cost of guest faculty from other departments

27. Which of the following statements concerning mandatory training is accurate?
    a. Administrative staff members are generally exempt from mandatory training
    b. Classroom style sessions of 15–30 minutes are most effective
    c. Attendance at mandatory training is critical to the safety of the organization
    d. Accrediting agencies do not allow mandatory training to be delivered as distance learning

28. Which of the following is an example of inservice training?
   a. A course on the pathophysiology of left hemisphere CVA
   b. A learning activity focusing on the action, side effects, and administration of newly approved chemotherapeutic agents
   c. A course preparing nurses for certification in neurology nursing
   d. A program dealing with the safe use of a new patient-controlled analgesia device

29. It is necessary to do all of the following when inservicing a new hospital policy EXCEPT:
   a. Maintain evidence that employees have read, comprehend, and will comply with the new policy
   b. Make sure that all employees have access to the new policy
   c. Develop a classroom presentation to discuss the new policy
   d. Include this activity as part of staff development efforts

30. When inservicing new equipment:
   a. It is not necessary to obtain the signature of the learner when documenting competency
   b. The instructor should document whether or not the learner is competent in the use of the equipment
   c. The staff development specialist does not need to keep a record of those who achieve competency
   d. The inservicing of new equipment is not an appropriate activity for the staff development specialist to become involved in

31. Continuing education in the classroom setting:
   a. Is not longer appropriate
   b. Relies on administrative or managerial support to increase attendance
   c. Should be offered primarily during the day shift
   d. Does not qualify for continuing education credits

32. The evaluation process is conducted primarily for the purpose of _____.
   a. Making sure that your learners enjoy themselves during learning activities
   b. Showing administration that the number of program participants increase every year
   c. Identifying evidence that links education to organizational effectiveness
   d. Satisfying Joint Commission requirements

33. Assessing learner satisfaction is carried out by performing _____ evaluation.
   a. Reaction
   b. Knowledge acquisition
   c. Results
   d. Impact

34. Reactive evaluation:
    a. Does not provide any evidence that will help you to improve your staff development practice
    b. Is sufficient when conducted without any other type of evaluation
    c. Provides data regarding learner perceptions
    d. Does not need to be conducted for distance-learning activities

35. To produce evidence that knowledge has been acquired, you must:
    a. Require that participants participate in a return demonstration at the conclusion of a learning activity
    b. Have all participants take and pass a written test at the conclusion of a learning activity
    c. Ask participants about their satisfaction with the program at its conclusion
    d. Have participants complete both a pretest prior to the learning activity and complete a posttest at the conclusion of the learning activity.

36. Evaluation of behavior can involve:
    a. Calculating the cost of equipment
    b. Scores on a posttest
    c. Learner satisfaction
    d. Observing a psychomotor skill in the actual work setting

37. Impact evaluation is:
    a. Documented evidence that knowledge has been acquired
    b. The process of demonstrating that a particular learning activity is linked to organizational results
    c. Only necessary if administration requests these types of data
    d. Focuses on the results of observed behavior in a classroom setting

38. ROI is calculated for:
    a. All learning activities
    b. Programs that do not affect knowledge acquisition
    c. Learning activities that significantly impact the organization's bottom line
    d. By the chief financial officer in your organization

39. When conducting ROI:
    a. Express findings in terms of a percentage
    b. Divide the program costs by its benefits
    c. Multiply the answer of the benefits divided by costs by 50
    d. Multiply the program costs by its benefits and divide by 100

Nursing education evaluation

Name: _____

Title: _____

Facility name: _____

Address: _____

Address: _____

City: _____ State: _____ ZIP: _____

Phone number: _____ Fax number: _____

E-mail: _____

Nursing license number: _____

(ANCC requires a unique identifier for each learner)

	Strongly disagree				Strongly agree

1. This activity met the following learning objectives:

a.) Described the historical evolution of staff development	1	2	3	4	5
b.) Differentiated between traditional and contemporary staff development practice	1	2	3	4	5
c.) Implemented strategic planning using mission, vision, and values statements	1	2	3	4	5
d.) Determined realistic departmental goals	1	2	3	4	5
e.) Determined realistic objectives that correlate with departmental goals	1	2	3	4	5
f.) Discussed the impact of current healthcare trends on staff development	1	2	3	4	5
g.) Described the facets of an organizational culture of learning	1	2	3	4	5
h.) Determined the appropriate qualifications for staff development specialists in an organization	1	2	3	4	5
i.) Identified staff development specialist competencies	1	2	3	4	5
j.) Described the various roles of the staff development specialist	1	2	3	4	5
k.) Implemented the principles of adult learning in all education activities	1	2	3	4	5
l.) Described characteristics of various learning styles	1	2	3	4	5
m.) Identified teaching strategies associated with various learning styles	1	2	3	4	5
n.) Described the characteristics of the four generations active in the current workforce	1	2	3	4	5
o.) Identified teaching strategies that facilitate learning for each generation	1	2	3	4	5
p.) Identified ways to design effective diversity education	1	2	3	4	5

		Strongly disagree				Strongly agree
q.)	Recognized education barriers that can cause resistance to learning	1	2	3	4	5
r.)	Implemented strategies to motivate the adult learner	1	2	3	4	5
s.)	Identified resourceful teaching strategies to improve education delivery	1	2	3	4	5
t.)	Implemented specific resourceful teaching strategies effectively	1	2	3	4	5
u.)	Differentiated among the various types of distance learning	1	2	3	4	5
v.)	Gathered evidence to select the most effective distance learning strategy	1	2	3	4	5
w.)	Determined teaching strategies using Benner's levels of competency as a framework	1	2	3	4	5
x.)	Correlated Benner's levels of clinical competency with staff development expertise	1	2	3	4	5
y.)	Described practical strategies to obtain needs-assessment data	1	2	3	4	5
z.)	Discussed orientation strategies that facilitate the orientee's organizational assimilation	1	2	3	4	5
aa.)	Discussed the concept of mandatory training	1	2	3	4	5
bb.)	Listed examples of inservice education	1	2	3	4	5
cc.)	Devised strategies for implementation of inservice education	1	2	3	4	5
dd.)	Discussed ways to deliver continuing education	1	2	3	4	5
ee.)	Identified the purposes of evaluation	1	2	3	4	5
ff.)	Described the various levels of the evaluation process	1	2	3	4	5
gg.)	Described level one evaluation	1	2	3	4	5
hh.)	Identified ways to measure level two evaluation	1	2	3	4	5
ii.)	Gathered evidence to evaluate behavior	1	2	3	4	5
jj.)	Described level four evaluation	1	2	3	4	5
kk.)	Described return on investment (ROI)	1	2	3	4	5
ll.)	Identified ways to conduct ROI	1	2	3	4	5

	Strongly disagree				Strongly agree
2. Objectives were related to the overall purpose/goal of the activity.	1	2	3	4	5
3. This activity was related to my nursing activity needs.	1	2	3	4	5
4. The exam for the activity was an accurate test of the knowledge gained.	1	2	3	4	5
5. The activity avoided commercial bias or influence.	1	2	3	4	5
6. This activity met my expectations.	1	2	3	4	5

7. Will this learning activity enhance your professional nursing practice?

❐ Yes   ❐ No

8. This educational method was an appropriate delivery tool for   **Strongly disagree**   **Strongly agree**

    the nursing/clinical audience.   1   2   3   4   5

9. How committed are you to making the behavioral changes suggested in this activity?

    a. Very committed   b. Somewhat committed   c. Not committed

10. Please provide us with your degree.

    a. ADN   b. BSN   c. MSN   d. Other, please state _____

11. Please provide us with your credentials.

    a. LVN   d. NP

    b. LPN   e. Other, please state

    c. RN

12. Providing nursing contact hours for this product influenced

    my decision to buy it.

13. I found the process to obtain my continuing education credits for

    this activity easy to complete.

14. If you did not find the process easy to complete, which of the following areas did you find

    the most difficult?

    a. Understanding the content of the activity

    b. Understanding the instructions

    c. Completing the exam

    d. Completing the evaluation

    e. Other, please state:

15. How much time did it take for you to complete this activity (this includes reading the book

    and completing the exam and the evaluation)? _____

16. If you have any comments on this activity, process, or selection of topics for nursing CE,

    please note them below.

_____

_____

_____

_____

17. Would you be interested in participating as a pilot tester for the development of future

    HCPro nursing education activities?

      ❐ Yes   ❐ No

Thank you for completing this evaluation of our nursing CE activity!